Regulation and Regulatory Reform

A Survey of Proposals
of the 95th Congress

American Enterprise Institute for Public Policy Research
Washington, D.C.

ISBN 0-8447-1079-2

Library of Congress Catalog Card No. 78-78060

Special Analysis No. 78-3

Printed in the United States of America

Price $2 per copy

CONTENTS

INTRODUCTION AND HIGHLIGHTS

Having been firmly established as an agenda item by the 94th Congress, regulatory reform became an even more popular topic for legislative proposals during the 95th Congress. Among items of lessening federal regulation, the most significant initiative was passage of the Airline Deregulation Act (P.L. 95-504). Also, the Natural Gas Policy Act (P.L. 95-621), whatever its short-term effects, contained a long-term deregulation component for new gas. Two proposals for partial deregulation (H.R. 13015 and H.R. 11611)—in the communications and drug field—also received considerable attention from the subcommittees with jurisdiction in these areas.

The activities of the 95th Congress in the regulatory field were not, however, limited to deregulation. Major new programs were enacted to

- prohibit American corporations from making payments to foreigners to influence official action (P.L. 95-213)
- impose environmental controls on strip mining (P.L. 95-87)
- provide new incentives for conservation of fossil fuels (P.L. 95-618) and increased reliance by commercial users on coal rather than oil or natural gas (P.L. 95-620).

A host of lesser measures increasing regulation were passed with respect to oil tanker safety (P.L. 95-474), outer continental shelf oil leasing (P.L. 95-372), ocean dumping (P.L. 95-153), uranium wastes (P.L. 95-604), nuclear material exports (P.L. 95-242), rabbit meat inspection (H.R. 2521; vetoed), domestic and foreign banking operations (P.L. 95-630 and P.L. 95-369), home heating insulation (P.L. 95-319), debt collection practices (P.L. 95-109), mine safety (P.L. 95-164), off-track betting (P.L. 95-515), utility pole hook-ups for cable television (P.L. 95-234), ocean shipping rebate penalties (H.R. 9518; vetoed), and specific industry favors such as beef import quotas (H.R. 11545; vetoed) and assurances that gas station owners receive their day in court (P.L. 95-297).

Aside from the measures mentioned above, opponents of regulation made more modest progress, gaining a delay in the enforcement of the ban on saccharin (P.L. 95-203), a modification of the endangered species law (P.L. 95-632), some relief for pesticide manufacturers confronting long delays in approval of their products (P.L. 95-396), relaxation of mandatory retirement rules (P.L. 95-256), and reimbursement for losses suffered by companies as a result of the 1977 ban on the sale of Tris-treated children's sleepwear (S. 1503; vetoed).

Perhaps the greatest success of those favoring increased reliance on the marketplace was the defeat of a variety of proposals of a regulatory type—for

1

example, labor law revision (H.R. 8410, S. 2467), common site picketing (H.R. 4250), agency for consumer advocacy (S. 1262, H.R. 9718), hospital cost containment (H.R. 6575, S. 1391), gun control (P.L. 95-429), no-fault automobile insurance (S. 1381, H.R. 13048), control of biological research in the DNA field (H.R. 11192), oil cargo preference for American tankers (H.R. 1037), regulation of the accounting profession (H.R. 13175), increased controls on pipelines carrying liquefied natural gas (H.R.11622, S. 1895), and rules for automatic telephone-dialing businesses (H.R. 9505, S. 2193).

Turning from substantive proposals to procedural ones, it is clear that an overwhelming majority of the members of the 95th Congress favored passage of some type of reform. But support was divided between reforms supported mainly by the business community and those supported mainly by the consumer movement. On the one hand, the reforms of high priority to business groups would have required cost/benefit assessments of regulatory proposals (H.R. 351), regulatory budgets (S. 3550, H.R. 14166), regulatory impact statements, (H.R. 10257), mandatory reductions in compliance costs (S. 3262, H.R. 14165), legislative vetoes (H.R. 959, S. 1463), and other procedures to reduce agency independence from the legislative and executive branches. On the other hand, the consumerists tended to favor reforms that would have increased agency independence from the White House, provided for greater access of consumer viewpoints to the agencies (agency for consumer advocacy, S. 1262, H.R. 6805) and to the courts (class action legislation, S. 3475), lessened anticompetitive regulations (S. 2625), reduced potential conflicts of interest (S. 3240), allowed more public participation (payment of attorney's fees, S. 270 and H.R. 3361), increased disclosure of lobbying activities (H.R. 8494), and toughened agency enforcement procedures (H.R. 3816).

Since support was somewhat divided among the various approaches within each camp, the result was that little regulatory reform legislation of a procedural nature was enacted into law. The only major achievements were the so-called ethics bill for financial disclosure by government officials in all branches of government (P.L. 95-521), and a bill to reform procedures of the Consumer Product Safety Commission (P.L. 95-631).

Generally, the Senate took more positive action than the House on procedural reforms, passing bills to require reauthorizations of almost all federal programs (Sunset, S. 2) and, as amendments to that proposal, have the President develop plans to eliminate conflicts among regulations of federal agencies and rank all federal programs as to their effectiveness. The Senate also passed bills to streamline the procedures and recodify the rules of the Federal Trade Commission (FTC) and four other independent agencies and to make enforcement more certain, reduce delay, and increase independence from the executive branch—all of which were matters of higher priority to the consumer movement (H.R. 3816, S. 1532, and S. 1534 through 1536). A similar measure to recodify the basic statutes of the independent agencies was passed (S. 263).

In actions of more interest to business concerns, particularly small ones, the Senate passed a bill to reauthorize the Small Business Administration which contained an exemption for small firms from most of the regulation of the Occupational Safety and Health Administration, or OSHA (H.R. 11445). It also passed the Regulatory Flexibility Act (S. 1974), encouraging all government agencies to treat small business differently when establishing regulations and enforcement schedules. In addition, as part of the S. Res. 4 proposals reorganizing the committee system at the beginning of the 95th Congress, the Senate passed an amendment to its rules requiring the committee report accompanying each bill to include a regulatory impact evaluation focusing on the likely economic, paperwork, and privacy impacts of the proposed law.

The House took action on only three of these bills. It reduced the OSHA exemption from the Small Business Administration bill to cover minor paperwork and inspection requirements before approving it, passed the FTC Amendments Act to reform that agency's procedures, and approved a less controversial reform bill concerning the Consumer Product Safety Commission (S. 2796, H.R. 12442). Conversely, the Senate did not act on the House-passed measure to require a broader approach to disclosure of lobby activities (H.R. 8494). Thus, again in the procedural area, opponents of regulation achieved more success in the form of preventing the adoption of regulatory reforms advocated by consumers than by rolling back existing regulations.

As this discussion suggests, the seeming consensus on the need for regulatory reform masked a substantial disagreement over what, in fact, was in need of reform. As mentioned above, there appeared to be two reasonably distinct movements: one oriented toward the concerns of consumer and environmental advocates, and the other oriented towards the concerns of the business community as a whole. In some cases these two movements supported the same legislative proposals. Price and route deregulation of airlines and surface transportation (trucks, railroads, and buses) were examples. Particular firms within these industries may have been opposed to deregulation, but the business community as a whole, being a consumer of these services, adopted the position of consumer advocates in favor of more price competition.

In some instances where conflicts existed but the priorities of the two sides differed, there was room for compromise. The proposals to partially deregulate the communications industry and reform drug regulation are cases in point. The communications bill (H.R. 13015) proposed by Representative Van Deerlin (D-Calif.) for example, would have both helped and hurt AT&T, local telephone companies, and broadcast stations. In the drug area, the administration's bill (H.R. 11611, S. 2755) would have made it easier for drug manufacturers to obtain initial approval to market new drugs but would also have made it easier for the FDA to withdraw unsafe drugs from the market.

Where there was conflict and no opportunity for compromise on the issue, each side simply went its own way, apparently hoping to build a majority or to arrange a horse-trade among different issues. For example, Senator Warren Magnuson (D-Wash.) tried to tie oil cargo preference for American tankers (H.R. 1037) to a bill increasing oil tanker safety (S. 682), but the House defeated the cargo preference bill before it could be offered.

In the analysis that follows, the framework just described will be helpful to the reader in understanding the regulatory and regulatory reform bills developed in the 95th Congress. Procedural bills will be addressed according to whether they *chiefly* addressed the reform concerns of the consumer and environmental advocates, or of the business community and those concerned with regulatory costs, or a combination of the two. Substantive bills will be addressed according to whether their overall thrust was to reduce the amount of regulation, to increase the amount of regulation, or to do some of both.

PROCEDURAL REFORMS

Proposals Supported Mainly by Business Groups

In the 95th Congress, a wide range of proposals were advanced to reduce the costs of regulation to businesses and other private parties. The major ones are discussed below. The legislative veto and other proposals designed in part to increase the general accountability of regulatory agencies to Congress are discussed separately.

Controlling Costs. *Economic impact statements.* The mildest set of proposals concerning costs was to give statutory underpinnings to the concept embodied in executive orders issued by both President Ford and President Carter to require agencies to prepare an economic analysis of their major regulatory proposals. The analysis was initially called an "inflation impact statement" and later an "economic impact statement" in the Ford years (Executive Orders 11821 and 11949), while the Carter administration (Executive Order 12044) changed its requirements somewhat and referred to it as a "regulatory analysis."

Representative Elliott Levitas (D-Ga.) was one of the first to call for statutory enactment of something like the Carter administration's regulatory analysis. Under a measure Levitas introduced December 7, 1977 (H.R. 10257), the official responsible for issuing a proposed rule would also be responsible for preparing a statement that would: analyze the rule's cost impact on consumers and businesses (including the direct and indirect costs of compliance); examine likely effects on employment, on productivity, on competition, and on supplies of important products; specify adverse impacts that could not be avoided; and analyze alternatives to the rule and tell why they were rejected.

Since the Carter executive order in its final form did not apply to the independent regulatory agencies (because of political opposition from some quarters in Congress and the agencies, and because of doubts about the constitutionality of such an extension), Senator Lloyd Bentsen (D-Tex.) and Representative Clarence Brown (R-Ohio), members of the Joint Economic Committee, introduced just prior to adjournment in October 1978 the Independent Agencies Regulatory Improvements Act of 1978 (S. 3549, H.R. 14369). This bill would have required that the independent agencies follow the same procedures in issuing regulations as are now required in the executive departments under the President's Executive Order. The Bentsen/Brown proposal was supported by the White House.

As previously noted, at the beginning of the 95th Congress the Senate amended its rules (Rule 29) to require the committee reports accompanying bills to contain a regulatory impact evaluation. This evaluation must estimate the bill's overall impact and also examine in detail the bill's effects on prices, privacy, and paperwork. Under the new rules, the Senate cannot consider a bill on the floor unless it has been provided such an evaluation (or an explanation of why such an evaluation is impractical). These rules were part of the Senate reorganization proposals (S. Res. 4) that were introduced by Senator Adlai Stevenson (D-Ill.) and fifteen others and adopted on February 4, 1977. The House had previously amended its Rule 11 to require a statement of inflationary impacts of proposed new laws. This requirement was part of the H.R. 988 proposals which took effect January 3, 1975.

To help Congress evaluate the regulatory analyses conducted by the executive branch, Representative Levitas, just prior to adjournment, introduced a bill (H.R. 14339) that would have established an Office of Regulatory Review in the General Accounting Office. The office would have prepared an evaluation of all economic impact statements issued by the executive branch. Senator Jacob Javits (R-N.Y.) had introduced a somewhat similar measure in the 94th Congress.

Presidential ranking of programs. The Government Accountability Act of 1978 was introduced in early August 1978 as S. 3366 by Senator Charles Percy (R-Ill.) and as H.R. 13723 by Representative William Steiger (R-Wis.). This bill would have required that the President submit to Congress at the beginning of each Congress a management report along with his budget message. The report would have ranked all programs within an executive or independent agency and also labeled them according to whether they were "excellent," "adequate," or "unsatisfactory." The effectiveness rankings would have been based on several criteria, including clarity of objectives, overall program design, and overall quality of program management. The President's reasons for his evaluations would also have been required as well as his recommendations for administrative or legislative improvements. The director of the Office of Management and Budget would also have been required to submit a report evaluating programs and noting those in the independent agencies contrary to federal policy.

The idea for the Percy/Steiger bill stems from a summer 1978 article by a former Ford administration official, Laurence H. Silberman, who argued that only by forcing the President to rank programs according to their effectiveness could publicity and popular support be generated to eliminate ineffective programs. The concept could easily have supplemented sunset proposals and, in fact, was added to the sunset bill as an amendment, which passed the Senate in October 1978.

Regulatory cost/benefit assessments. At the beginning of the 95th Congress several bills were introduced in the House to require a regulatory cost/benefit assessment for each regulation and each piece of legislation that was proposed by an "agency of the federal Government" and that would have a "significant impact on costs." As an example, the Regulatory Cost Impact Act (H.R. 351), sponsored by Representative Samuel Devine (R-Ohio), would have required agencies to perform a comprehensive assessment of "reasonably foreseeable" costs and benefits, to estimate the net public benefit, and to examine "reasonable" alternatives. The cost/benefit assessment would have had to consider effects that would be short-run *or* long-run, direct *or* indirect, and quantifiable *or* nonquantifiable. A draft assessment would have been submitted for public comment and also for evaluation by the Office of Management and Budget. A final assessment (with any amendments added after an additional public comment period) would have been attached to the regulation when published in the *Federal Register*. Emergency procedures would have allowed an agency to issue a new regulation without an assessment if the delay would have "presented a substantial risk to the health and safety of persons or to national security," if the regulation was accompanied by a statement on how the risk was determined, and if the draft assessment was completed within sixty days. The President would have issued guidelines for the cost/benefit assessment process within 120 days after enactment. Upon written request by "any interested party," existing regulations would have had to be reviewed for substantial excesses of costs over benefits. If such excesses were found to exist, the regulation would have had to be altered. The assessment process would also have been applied to legislation reported by committees in Congress, thus a variation of amended Senate Rule 29 would have been enacted into law. The validity of the cost/benefit assessments would have been judicially reviewable, just as environmental impact statements are now.

Regulatory compliance costs budgets. Senator Bentsen has been the leading member of Congress in proposing bills that would set specific goals on limiting the compliance costs of regulation. His first bill, the Regulatory Cost Reduction Act of 1978 (S. 3262), introduced June 29, 1978, and cosponsored in the House by Rep. Clarence Brown (H.R. 14165), would have required that before the start of each fiscal year for the next five years the executive departments and independent agencies submit a regulatory cost report to the President, the Congress, and the comptroller general. This report would have contained (1) a breakdown of actual or projected costs of compliance for each existing or proposed regulation in the previous year, present year, and coming year; (2) a discussion of actions planned or implemented in those three years to reduce compliance costs, with those actions aiming to reduce compliance costs by at least 5 percent per year; (3) a list of laws that impose "excessively high" costs of compliance; and (4) a statement explaining any failures to achieve the 5 percent goal. However, the bill included no provisions to penalize agencies that fail to meet either that goal or any of the bill's other "requirements."

The bill would have given the President responsibility to establish criteria for determining which rules and regulations would be covered by the cost-review system and also to develop methods for accurately and uniformly calculating costs of compliance. The methods proposed by the President would have been subject to public comment and would have been reviewed by his economic and management advisers. On or before March 30 for each of the five years, the President and the head of each agency would have prepared and transmitted to Congress a report containing recommendations to reduce the projected costs of compliance of federal regulation by 5 percent that year. The recommendations would have utilized eight suggested methods of compliance-cost reduction relating to paperwork elimination, the substitution of performance standards for design standards, the increased use of market incentives, and the termination of outdated rules. The recommendations would have been subjected to a sixty-day, two-house legislative veto. To assist with the legislative review, the comptroller general would have submitted an evaluation of the recommendations within thirty days to the Congress.

Senator Bentsen's second bill (S. 3550), introduced in October 1978 and again introduced in the House by Rep. Clarence Brown (H.R. 14370), would have implemented the regulatory-budget concept, which has received some attention from Secretary of Commerce Juanita Kreps. Under the terms of this proposal, a budget for maximum allowable regulatory compliance costs in a given year would be prepared and submitted to Congress by the President along with the regular budget. Prior to this, each agency would submit to the President a report containing (1) a proposed regulatory budget with justifications, (2) a breakdown of the previous fiscal year's compliance costs, and (3) an explanation for any costs which exceeded the previous year's budget. The comptroller general would evaluate these reports for the Congress. If the President's proposed budget for any agency were lower than an agency's estimated total compliance costs, the President in his budget message would have had to recommend specific actions to reduce these costs.

Senator Bentsen's second bill directed the President to oversee the development of appropriate methodologies to implement the system in a manner identical to that in Senator Bentsen's first bill. The timetable for developing each regulatory budget would have been as follows:

- November 10 preceding a fiscal year—the agencies submit their compliance-cost budgets to the President and Congress
- day of regular budget message to Congress—President submits his regulatory budget to Congress
- May 15—comptroller general submits his evaluation of agency budgets
- July 15—each standing committee of the House and Senate submits to the budget committees its views and estimates of maximum compliance costs
- August 15—budget committees report concurrent resolution establishing the regulatory budget
- September 15—Congress completes action on the regulatory budget for each agency.

Any legislation which increased compliance costs after Congress had completed action on the concurrent resolution would not have been allowed unless the budget committees provided a waiver.

Presidential authority to delay implementation of rules. According to a proposal first outlined by Washington attorneys Lloyd Cutler and David Johnson in a *Yale Law Review* article, the President should be given the power to order an agency to consider or reconsider a proposed major regulation when he finds that the purpose of the regulation conflicts with some other congressionally mandated policy goal of high priority. Although this proposal has yet to be introduced in Congress, Senator Thomas McIntyre (D-N.H.) took the first small step toward discretionary presidential authority to affect rules by introducing the Red Tape Reduction Act (S. 1199), which he filed March 31, 1977. Senator McIntyre's proposal would have allowed the President, upon the request of an agency head, to delay for up to one year the effective date required by law for the promulgation of rules if additional time was required to collect data or consult with affected parties. This provision would have delayed law suits brought by parties who wanted immediate compliance regardless of the costs. Other sections of the bill proposed procedural changes concerning the notice and comment period to make rulemaking more responsive to the public. Such changes will be discussed in a later section of this work.

Exemptions from regulation. Senators Gaylord Nelson (D-Wis.) and John Culver (D-Iowa) moved to protect the interests of small business on August 1, 1977, by introducing the Regulatory Flexibility Act (S. 1974), which would have allowed agencies to issue two versions of a regulation, one intended for small business and the other for larger firms. As passed by the Senate on October 15, 1978, it would have empowered agencies ''to issue rules or regulation which apply differently to different segments of the regulated population'' and required agencies to ''solicit and consider alternative regulatory proposals from the public prior to the adoption of final rules.''

The rulemaking body would have had to consider establishment of: differing requirements for compliance and reporting, differing timetables for compliance, exemptions coverage, and simplification of requirements. It would also have had to explain in detail what purposes each paperwork requirement would serve. Within 180 days after enactment each agency would have had to publish a plan for review of already existing regulations from these perspectives. A set of seven criteria was provided to help in evaluating such rules.

During floor debate on August 2, 1978, the Senate added to the Small Business Administration's authorization bill (H.R. 11445, sponsored by Neal Smith and seventeen cosponsors) an exemption from the requirements of the Occupational Safety and Health Act. No such exemption existed in the House version. The conference committee reached a compromise which prohibited OSHA from fining businesses that have ten or fewer employees and that were found to have committed ten or fewer violations in first inspection. (However, OSHA would not be prohibited from fining any firms guilty of certain ''serious'' violations.) The compromise also exempted such businesses from existing OSHA rules that require firms to keep logs and to prepare annual reports on all occupational injuries and illnesses unless they participate in statistical surveys. For reasons other than disagreement with these provisions, the President vetoed the bill.

Increasing Accountability. *Legislative veto of agency rules.* The concept of the legislative veto is that Congress or a part of Congress (one house or one committee) should have the opportunity for a specified period of time to veto an executive agency action before it takes effect. During the 1970s, Congress has increasingly imposed legislative veto requirements, partly because of skepticism that arose from presidential handling of the Vietnam War and partly because from 1969 through 1976 the party that controlled Congress did not control the presidency. Legislative vetoes were first used in 1932, and they have appeared in at least 135 pieces of legislation through 1977 and were applied to 176 types of regulation.[1] In most cases, such vetoes are applied to executive actions, but beginning around 1972 they have been applied in more cases of agency rulemaking. In the 95th Congress many attempts were made in committee to attach legislative veto provisions to bills dealing with rulemaking agencies, but they were often defeated by committee majorities that approved of the general direction in which agency policies were moving. The Democratic leadership of the House and Senate and most committee chairmen oppose the use of legislative vetoes in most rulemaking situations. However, there is a good deal of support in the House as a whole for use of legislative vetoes in rulemaking cases. This is one reason why the FTC Amendments Act (H.R. 3816) became a good vehicle for legislative veto advocates when it reached the House floor. The House twice defeated the conference report when the conferees refused to leave the legislative-veto provision in the bill. Legislative-veto provisions which applied to rulemaking were attached to at least four other major pieces of legislation during floor debate in the House in the 95th Congress, although they were all dropped in conference. The bills involved were the Hatch Act reforms, the pesticide registration reforms, the HUD reauthorization bill, and the measure establishing the Department of Energy.

The concept of the veto is very controversial for several reasons. With the exception of reorganization bills, presidents find it generally to be an encroachment on their executive power although it is not clear in the case of rulemaking by the independent agencies that executive power rather than legislative power is involved. There are doubts about the legislative veto's constitutionality, insofar as it may violate the separation of powers. Opponents of the legislative veto note that it can increase delays in rulemaking and that it may unduly divert Congress from broader, more important policy decisions. Opponents also claim that, when applied to rulemaking agencies, the congressional veto may lead these agencies to make greater use of adjudication techniques in an effort to avoid the veto. There are additional objections to the single-committee and one-house veto on the grounds that they are too narrow and do not represent the views of the majority. Some good questions have been raised about what would happen if each house of Congress vetoed part of a regulation rather than the whole, especially if it were not the same part. These latter two issues can be dealt with by prohibiting certain kinds of vetoes. But opponents have two additional objections which are more fundamental. First, the congressional veto is considered a tool which allows special interests to evade the agency prohibitions against *ex parte* contacts to influence policy. Second, the vetoes defeat the purpose of delegating rulemaking powers from generalist politicians to independent experts.

Advocates of the congressional veto respond that the independence theory of rulemaking is outdated and that political judgments about conflicting societal goals are an essential part of the rulemaking process and should not go unreviewed. Defenders of the veto would prefer to have the politics which inevitably surround rulemaking take place in public rather than in the less visible agency arena. It is further noted that members of Congress are capable of getting expertise from many sources to inform their decisions and that deference to expertise on some technical issues is just as much a part of the agency rulemaking process as it is of the legislative process. In addition, it is noted that legislative vetoes increase accountability to the public and may make agencies more responsive without the veto ever having to be exercised. Supporters also dispute the contention that rulemaking is executive power rather than delegated legislative power. They further consider the sixty- or ninety-day delay in implementation of rules to be trivial compared with other delays. Finally, they note that as of 1976 there have not been that many resolutions introduced in Congress calling for an exercise of the veto (only 732 between 1960 and mid-1978) and only a small number of these (81) were ever adopted.[2]

Regardless of the merits of the concept, the legislative veto has substantial support in Congress. The leading set of proposals for an across-the-board legislative veto has 185 cosponsors in the House, and a majority of the House was twice willing to vote against its leadership and the Carter administration on the FTC veto issue. Also, in the 94th Congress a bill with an across-the-board legislative veto of agency rules was reported by the House Judiciary Committee and, when the Rules Committee did not clear the bill for floor consideration, the bill fell only two votes short of the two-thirds vote necessary for passage under suspension of the rules. Many states have experimented successfully with the veto,[3] and support in Congress is greatest among junior members of the House who often have served in state legislatures and who are thus less attached to previous federal programs. The fact that turnover among House seats previously held by senior members remains high this year suggests that the next Congress may be even more favorably inclined to impose legislative vetoes on the floor if they fail in committee.

A number of virtually identical bills carrying the title Administrative Rule Making Reform Act of 1977 and imposing a legislative veto on agency rulemaking were introduced on the first day of the 95th Congress. The one ending with most publicity and support was H.R. 959 sponsored by the House's leading advocate of the veto, Elliott Levitas (D-Ga.). This measure was identical to the one reported by the House Judiciary Committee in the 94th Congress and applied to existing as well as future rules. Companion bills H.R. 960 and H.R. 961 were less broad in scope. H.R. 960 applied only to future regulations. H.R. 961 applied only to regulations which carry penalties of fines, imprisonment, loss of federal funds, or civil penalties for noncompliance. Together with other identical legislative veto bills the Levitas approach has 185 cosponsors.

The veto procedure was the same in all three bills. After a new rule was promulgated it would not become effective (1) if within 90 days of continuous session of Congress both houses adopted a concurrent resolution of disapproval or reconsideration, or (2) if within 60 days of continuous session, one house adopted such a resolution and it was not disapproved by the other house within 30 days thereafter, or it would become effective if at the end of 60 days no committee of either house had reported or been discharged from further consideration of such a resolution. Agencies had 180 days to revise regulations after a reconsideration resolution was passed, otherwise such rules would have lapsed. A new category of emergency regulations addressed to problems of immediate importance got around the veto but expired after 210 days. An almost identical measure was introduced by

Walter Flowers (D-Ala.) in the House (H.R. 116) and Sam Nunn (D-Ga.) in the Senate (S. 1463), while Rep. Del Clawson (R-Calif.) sponsored a somewhat similar bill (H.R. 4901). All of these bills also contained provisions to increase opportunities for public notice of agency rulemaking and for public participation in a way that appealed to regulated parties, particularly small businesses. Most of the legislative veto bills also contained a sunset provision terminating the legislative veto of rulemaking after a four-year experiment. The Levitas version also contained a clause which stated that failure of Congress to pass a resolution of disapproval did not affect the right of anyone to challenge a rule in the courts.

Several other measures containing legislative-veto provisions were introduced in the Senate. S. 2862, the Regulatory Control Act, sponsored by Senator Floyd Haskell (D-Colo.) and three cosponsors, would have subjected every rule promulgated pursuant to the Administrative Procedures Act to review every five years under a veto provision and required all new legislation reported out of committee to have one of five forms of legislative veto apply to rules issued pursuant to it. S. 2011, which was introduced August 4, 1977, by Senator Harrison Schmitt (R-N.Mex.) with five cosponsors and filed in the House (H.R. 11006) by Rep. Bill Archer (R-Tex.), would have required each rule subject to the legislative veto to be accompanied by economic, paperwork, and judicial impact analyses, limited the life of most rules to five years unless repromulgated, and subjected rules with specified penalties and economic impacts to a two-house mandatory approval process rather than a one-house veto process.

Looking to the future, one of the more controversial proposals may be Senator Schmitt's redraft of S. 2011, which he introduced near adjournment as S. 3629. Patterned on the process used in several states, it would create a Joint Committee on Administrative Rules to oversee the legislative veto process and review the economic impact and cost/benefit reports required to be submitted with the rule. The joint committee would report resolutions of disapproval when it found that costs exceeded benefits or that the rule was unwise public policy from several perspectives. Rep. Tom Kindness (R-Ohio) introduced a similar measure in the House (H.R. 14222) right before adjournment. A joint committee approach has been discussed before in Congress and usually draws heavy opposition from authorizing committee chairmen who would lose some of their oversight power because this approach detaches part of the oversight process from those committees associated with a program area.

Expansion of public notice and comment, and public participation. Public participation is usually regarded as something which primarily concerns so-called public interest organizations such as consumer and environmental groups. It is true that certain reforms in the public participation area, such as government payment of attorney's fees for those who represent diffuse interests, are given a high priority by consumer advocates. However, other reforms in this area are also of concern to small businesses and other members of the general public who feel the major paperwork or economic impacts of regulations. The latter groups may not be able to afford or may not have access to the legal representatives and lobbyists of large corporations or public interest groups who keep these organizations informed about pending developments in government. It is not surprising to find broad reforms that affect these information and participation areas attached to bills which also carry legislative vetoes of agency regulations, including the proposals of Representatives Levitas and Flowers and Senator Nunn. Since both the American Bar Association and the Administrative Conference of the United States have endorsed some narrower procedural reforms in these fields, the Administrative Law Subcommittee of the House Judiciary Committee and the Administrative Practice and Procedure Subcommittee of the Senate Judiciary Committee have both taken an active interest in the subject and held hearings on the matter in the 94th Congress.

In June 1977, Senator James Abourezk (D-S. Dak.), chairman of the relevant Senate subcommittee, introduced legislation (S. 1721) at the request of the American Bar Association and the Administrative Conference to implement their limited reforms along with some others dealing with problems of delay. The Abourezk bill would have greatly narrowed the broad military and foreign-affairs exemption to the requirement of the Administrative Procedures Act that agencies publish notice of proposed rulemaking and give opportunity for public comment. However, the bill retained the "good cause" exemption that would still allow an agency to omit notice and comment if it found that these would be "impractical, unnecessary, or contrary to the public interest" and if a statement to this effect were attached to the document issuing the rule.

The Abourezk bill would also have eliminated the so-called proprietary exemption from notice and comment which covers rulemaking relating to "public property, loans, grants, benefits, or contracts" as it is conducted by federal agencies (such as the Bureau of Land Management, the Small Business Administration, the National Science Foundation, the Department of Transportation, and the General Services Administration). Most agencies voluntarily give notice and comment already on rules concerning grants, but the government contracts field is more complicated. The Abourezk bill also contained other provisions which protected the rights of affected parties under expedited rate-making and licensing procedures.

The participation reforms in the legislative veto bills (H.R. 116, H.R. 959, and S. 1463), the Administrative Rule Making Reform Act of 1977, were somewhat broader in scope. In addition to publishing in the *Federal Register* a notice of intention to regulate, agencies would have had to "make a reasonable attempt to inform those likely to be affected by the proposed rulemaking or, if the group was large, representative members" of the group, presumably through notices in trade journals. At present, some agencies do one or the other but not both. Copies of the notice of proposed rulemaking would also have had to be sent to all persons requesting it.

Moreover, the specifics of what must be in the notice were laid out more fully. The "good cause" exemptions to notice and comment were also more specific. In addition to restricting the definition of military and foreign policy exemptions, notice and comment would have been unnecessary if the rule were of "routine nature" or of "insignificant impact" or where a new category of "emergency" rules (which expired in 210 days) would have prevented delay that could (1) "seriously injure an important public interest," (2) "substantially frustrate legislative policies,'' or (3) ''seriously damage a person or class of persons without serving any important public interest.'' At the time of issuance of an emergency rule, public rulemaking proceedings would have commenced while under present procedures they are skipped altogether. The new language further qualified the exemptions by stating that they did not preclude inviting persons representing different viewpoints from submitting ideas or creating an advisory committee.

In addition, the minimum period of time for public comment for rules was set at forty-five days (the Administrative Procedures Act had previously said a ''reasonable period''), and the agency was required to keep in its file for each rulemaking proceeding ''copies of petitions for exceptions to, amendments of, or repeal of a rule.'' The file would have been available to the courts, Congress, and the public. After the rule was adopted, a special statement setting forth the ''primary considerations imposed by persons outside the agency in opposition to the rule'' would have been included along with reasons for rejecting these considerations. If, in issuing a rule, the agency deviated from the procedures set forth in the new law, no person could have been penalized for violating the rule.

Other provisions of the Administrative Rule Making Reform Act specified the criteria to be used in selecting procedures to handle significant factual controversies. The formal adjudication procedures of the Administrative Procedures Act (5 U.S.C. 556 and 557) were not required unless the law establishing the regulations called for ''on the record proceedings after opportunity for agency hearing.'' The courts have already required formal hearings where ''on the record'' rulemaking is called for, but the bill's choice of the full adjudication model of sections 556 and 557 went somewhat beyond what most courts have required.

A somewhat related bill, H.R. 5633, sponsored by Rep. Tom Kindness (R-Ohio) would have set the minimum public comment period at sixty days and, upon the request of an interested party, allowed a thirty-day extension of the comment period, unless such an extension was ruled to be contrary to the public interest. This measure also contained provisions terminating the proprietary exemption and making the other changes suggested in the proposed Administrative Rule Making Reform Act.

Another measure for ending the proprietary exemption (H.R. 2416) was introduced by Rep. Ronald Dellums (D-Calif.). In addition, it would have waived the government's immunity from lawsuits that claim officials failed to act in an official capacity or under color of law if the suits were for other than money damages. The Dellums bill also contained a provision for government payment of attorney's fees and would have established procedures to handle complaints from persons or organizations accused of failing to comply with the terms of grants-in-aid.

Another proposal (H.R. 2586) sponsored by Tom Hagedorn (R-Minn.) was of special interest to the business community. It contained a provision that would have awarded attorney's fees and other costs to any defendant in a civil action in which the government was the plaintiff and lost.

The standard bills establishing government payment of attorney's fees to public participants in agency rulemaking are discussed below in the section on measures of high priority to the consumer movement.

Proposals Supported Mainly by Consumer Groups

Restructuring the Regulatory Appointments Process. *Broad representation mandates.* One of the major recommendations contained in the regulatory reform study by the Senate Government Affairs Committee was for the President and Congress to ensure that regulatory commission memberships are well balanced. This would include broad representation of various talents, backgrounds, occupations, and experience appropriate to the functions of each commission. This very language formed the basis of section 4 of the Independent Regulatory Commission Act (S. 3240), sponsored by Senator John Glenn (R-Ohio) and cosponsored by Senators Charles Percy (R-Ill.) and Abraham Ribicoff (D-Conn.), along with a statement that commissioners should be individuals who are qualified by reason of training, education, or experience. A similar mandate existed in Senator Ribicoff's proposal (S. Res. 258), cosponsored by Senators Percy and Javits, to expand the investigative procedures used to check presidential appointments.

Independent selection process. In his Regulatory Agency Appointment Reform Act (H.R. 3518), Rep. Abner Mikva (D-Ill.) went one step further and would have required the establishment of a Federal Regulatory Agency Nominating Board, composed of fifteen presidentially appointed members, of which only eight could be from the same political party. After hearings the board would forward to the White House three names qualified to fill a vacancy on a commission, and the President would have been required to pick one of the three. The board would have had to select names so as to ensure that at all times the majority of commissioners of any agency were individuals who in the preceding three years had not been "employed by, received substantial profits, fees, or wages from, or represented in a professional capacity, an industry or organization regulated by or directly affected by the regulatory activities of any regulatory agency." Reappointment of commissioners would have been prohibited, and former commissioners would have been prevented from practicing before their former agencies for two years.

It would also have been mandatory that a majority of the nominating board members be persons who were "representatives of the public at large" and thus met a three-year requirement of financial noninvolvement with the regulated industry. In addition, they would have to have demonstrated a "commitment to the public interest through membership in a civic, social, charitable, educational, or similar public-spirited organization or associations, or through employment by an agency of government or by a not-for-profit organization or other public oriented institution." Strict financial disclosure by the board members would also have been required.

Expanded investigation procedures of nominees. Senator Ribicoff, chairman of the Senate Government Affairs Committee, introduced with Senators Percy and Javits S. Res. 258 on September 8, 1977. This measure would have established a Senate Office of Nominations to investigate nominees for appointment to positions requiring the advice and consent of the Senate. It would also have put into Senate rules a "balanced representation" clause concerning regulatory appointments. The office would have collected biographical and financial data and investigated reports by federal and local officials. Also, the President would have had to submit to the office a report stating his reasons for each appointment. Within fifteen days after receiving these materials, the office would have confidentially reported on the results of the inquiry to the appropriate Senate committee indicating any conflicts of interest if they existed. The committees would have retained the right to conduct their own investigations if they so desired. In addition, Senate Rule 38 would have been amended to state that in considering nominees, the Senate would have to take into account whether they were qualified in terms of (1) background, training, and experience; (2) personal and professional integrity and a lack of conflicts of interest; (3) the nature of "the needs" of the particular office; and (4) the existing composition of that body in which "members of a single sector or group [might be] too heavily represented."

Although the Ribicoff proposal received much publicity, it encountered opposition from several committee chairmen who felt that it would interfere with their own prerogatives in one way or another or overly sacrifice the nominees' privacy, since items such as original FBI reports and tax returns would have been in the hands of the office. The resolution was never adopted, although the Government Affairs Committee did pass new rules for its own investigations of nominees for appointment to executive offices.

Increased Independence from the Executive Branch. *Prohibiting political clearance of staff.* The aforementioned Independent Regulatory Commission Act (S. 3240), sponsored by Senator Glenn, with Senators Percy and Ribicoff, contained a section which stated that no officers of independent commissions shall be indirectly or directly reviewed or approved except by the Civil Service Commission. The purpose of this wording was to prevent White House interference in the staff appointment process. The preamble to the bill also spoke of the need to insulate the commissions from "improper influence by the executive branch or private interests subject to regulation." A similar provision existed in S. 1288, sponsored by Wendell Ford (D-Ky.), to expand Federal Trade Commission powers; it passed in the Senate when S. 1288 was added to another bill (S. 1533) on the floor before passage.

Increasing congressional access to information. The Senate Commerce Committee reported and the Senate passed a series of "interim regulatory reform" bills dealing with individual commissions. These bills, sponsored by Senator Magnuson, were called the 1530 series because of their consecutive numbering from S. 1532 to S. 1537. They were originally part of an omnibus regulatory reform bill (S. 263), cosponsored by Senators Magnuson and James Pearson (R-Kans.), which would have required recodification and review of regulatory agency *laws* (the Interim Regulatory Reform Act of 1977). This omnibus bill was introduced in May 1977 and was also passed in the Senate. The 1530 series would have had the individual commissions recodify their *rules* over a period lasting 660 days. However, the individual interim reform bills also contained several provisions relating to agency independence. Both the 1530 series and Senator Glenn's S. 3240 would have forbidden the independent agencies from clearing with the administration any legislative recommendations, testimony, or comments on proposed legislation or budget requests or estimates. When this information was voluntarily submitted to the White House, copies would have had to be sent to Congress. The interim reform bills also called for all the independent agencies to submit documents to Congress within ten days of any written request for them. All of the 1530 series passed the Senate except S. 1533 (H.R. 3816 was substituted) and S. 1537 (postponed because of passage of the airline deregulation bill).

Independent authority to litigate. Both the interim reform bills and S. 3240 also gave the regulatory commissions more authority to bring civil actions independent of the Justice Department. The 1530 series would have given the Justice Department forty-five days after receipt of information of a violation to bring its own action with the commissions receiving authority to seek temporary injunctions immediately. Senator Glenn's measure had no forty-five-day waiting period.

Presidential appointment of chairmen. Although the President now appoints the chairmen of most commissions, the 1530 series and S. 3240 made it an across-the-board requirement and also made the advice and consent of the Senate mandatory. In addition, the interim reform bills would only have allowed the chairman to serve in that capacity "at the pleasure of the President" while Senator Glenn's bill restated the restrictions on the presidential power of removal which the courts have already imposed.

Reducing the Power of Special Interests. *Controlling the revolving-door pattern.* The tendency of some agencies to recruit commissioners from among those persons who work for or represent a regulated industry is not surprising since they have the expertise needed to be commissioners. However, there is some concern that a potential conflict of interest exists, since many former commissioners return to the same industry (or accept employment there for the first time) immediately after serving as a regulator of that industry. This so-called revolving-door pattern of recruitment is the subject of provisions in several regulatory reform bills. Both the 1530 series and S. 3240 restricted the employment of former commissioners, as did the Ethics in Government Act of 1978 (S. 555), which established standards for financial disclosure of top government officials and was signed by the President on October 26, 1978 (P.L. 95-521).

Senator Glenn's measure (S. 3240) would have restricted for one year both former commissioners and top staff (GS-16 and above) from appearing before or making any written or oral communications with commission personnel on *any* matter before them. It would also have prevented former commissioners from accepting employment in a firm directly or indirectly affected by the commission on which he or she served during the remainder of an incompleted term. The interim reform bills applied the general no-involvement restriction for two years and to personnel at the GS-15 level and above. They also restricted outside employment during service on a commission but contained no provision about noninvolvement during incompleted terms.

The Ethics in Government Act was more complex. It permanently prohibited involvement by former employees and their partners in any matter in which they

17

had a "direct and substantial interest and in which they participated personally and substantially." It also imposed a two-year prohibition on involvement with matters "under his [or her] official responsibility" within a period of one year prior to his or her termination and a one-year prohibition on any matters pending before his [or her] former agency. The penalties for violations were also listed and included a maximum of two years in prison and a $10,000 fine plus an additional ban on practice before that agency for as much as five years.

Financial disclosure. The provisions of the newly enacted Ethics Act cover all legislative, judicial, and executive branch officials and top staff. Relevant here is a requirement that all executive branch employees whose jobs require Senate confirmation (including regulatory commissioners) must file publicly available financial-disclosure reports within five days after their nomination; while those not subject to Senate confirmation would have thirty days to do so. The statement must include the source, type, and amount of earned income and honorarium from any source; the source, type, and general amount of unearned income during the preceding calendar year; and gifts, reimbursements, debts, real property, and certain income and holdings of spouses. The requirements of a qualified blind trust are established, and the attorney general may bring civil actions against violators of a blind trust agreement. The act establishes an Office of Government Ethics to develop rules and monitor and investigate compliance in the executive branch. Members of Congress, their stop staffs, and candidates must comply with similar rules with compliance monitored by the General Accounting Office. The financial disclosure provisions are the same as those previously adopted by Congress as part of its rules with civil penalties now available to enforce them. A section providing criminal penalties for all three branches of government was dropped from the bill in the House prior to passage, and an amendment repealing the 15 percent limit ($8,625) on outside earned income for members of Congress (which is part of the rules of the House and Senate) was also defeated.

Lobbying disclosure. In July 1977, House Judiciary Committee Chairman Peter Rodino (D-N.J.) and five cosponsors introduced the Public Disclosure of Lobbying Act (H.R. 8494), which would have replaced the 1946 Federal Regulation of Lobbying Act controlling registration and disclosure of lobbying activities. The proposed new law was eventually reported and passed by the House on April 26, 1978, despite considerable controversy about certain amendments added on the floor. However, the Senate Government Affairs Committee could not reach agreement on how strong a bill to report so the bill died in the Senate. The House bill, as passed, was less stringent than a version passed in the 94th Congress.

The heart of the lobbying bill called for registration with the comptroller general, that would be publicly available, by all organizations that expended $2,500 per quarter or which employed at least one individual who spent all or part of thirteen days to lobby. The registration would have had to be updated annually and the names of lobbyists would have had to be included. The reporting organization would also have had to describe certain activities each quarter including: (1) a list of lobbying expenditures including each one over $35 to a government employee; (2)

known business contacts with the person whom each organization is attempting to influence; and (3) the issues involved in the lobbying.

Two amendments supported by most public interest groups and opposed by most business groups were added on the floor before passage. Although they were included in the measure as it passed the House, they destroyed the fragile coalition supporting the bill. The first was a provision sponsored by Representative Flowers requiring registered organizations to report their grass roots lobbying activities (so-called lobbying solicitations) if they were addressed to 500 or more people, twenty-five or more employees, or twelve or more affiliates. Specifically to be disclosed were: the issue involved, of the means of solicitation, and the names of persons retained to make the solicitation. This amendment was aimed at the growing computerized mailing field. Paid advertisements costing more than $5,000 were also covered. The second amendment, offered by Rep. Tom Railsback (R-Ill.), would have forced disclosure of the names of organizations that gave $3,000 or more to a lobbying organization if that organization spent more than 1 percent of its total budget on lobbying. This section was aimed at disclosing that certain organizations with civic-minded titles received their principal funding from corporate sources. A similar amendment directed at major individual contributors was defeated on the grounds that it would discourage the defense of unpopular causes.

Other provisions of the bill would have authorized the attorney general to investigate alleged violations, to use informal methods to correct violations, and, if necessary, to institute civil or criminal actions against transgressors. Civil penalties of up to $10,000 and criminal penalties of $10,000 and two years imprisonment were provided for violators who knowingly failed to comply.

Increased agency powers. The interim regulatory reform bill concerning the Federal Trade Commission (S. 1533) differed from the other 1530 series bills, because another more controversial measure (S. 1288), sponsored by Wendell Ford (D-Ky.), which increased FTC powers and authorized appropriations was added to it as an amendment on the floor before passage. A similar authorization bill increasing FTC powers was passed in the House (H.R. 3816), filed by Bob Eckhardt (D-Tex.). Because of the unwillingness of House and Senate conferees to accept the House-passed provision for a legislative veto of FTC rules, the House twice defeated the conference report, and the bill died. Both versions of the bill provided for fines of up to $5,000 per day for failure to respond to the commission's subpoenas and orders after a thirty-day grace period for appeals. Another provision would have prohibited court challenges to FTC actions until the agency had begun enforcement, so the agency would be able to negotiate for information and consolidate law suits.

A third provision made cease-and-desist orders effective sixty days after issuance and allowed a court, on appeal of the order, to postpone only that part of the order that was challenged. A fourth section allowed the courts to appoint trustees to prevent a firm from ''siphoning away'' its assets while under FTC investigation. The bill also would have slightly increased FTC jurisdiction over matter affecting interstate commerce. Another section would have required the

FTC to respond within four months to petitions for issuance of a new rule or repeal of an old one. The most controversial part of the bill, an authorization for class action suits by outside groups harmed by violations of FTC rules, was dropped after strong business opposition.

Another reform bill that affected agency powers to a greater extent than the 1530 series was S. 2796, filed by Senators Wendell Ford and Warren Magnuson and its House counterpart, H.R. 12442, sponsored by Bob Eckhardt and five cosponsors, which concerned the Consumer Product Safety Commission (CPSC). The bill authorized a revision of rules of the CPSC, reformed operations to increase the effectiveness of the voluntary standards process, allowed private suits against CPSC employees for gross negligence, and toughened the regulations against exporting products that fail to meet U.S. safety standards. The bill was not as controversial as the one dealing with the FTC. It passed both houses and was signed into law (P.L. 95-631).

Increasing the Power of Consumer Interests. *Agency for consumer advocacy.* Arguing that the interests of consumers are too diffuse to be adequately represented by conventional lobbies, consumer advocates have tried to create a consumer lobby within the government. In every Congress since the 91st, at least one branch of Congress has passed a bill to create an agency for consumer advocacy. The Senate passed such measures in 1970 and 1975, and the House adopted the proposal in 1971, 1974, and 1975 despite diminishing support each time. When President Ford threatened a veto of the bill in the 94th Congress, the Democratic leadership of Congress let the measure die rather than holding a conference and sending the bill to the White House. In the 95th Congress, H.R. 6805, sponsored by Representative Jack Brooks (D-Tex.), and S. 1262, sponsored by Senator Abraham Ribicoff (D-Conn.), had the support of the White House for the first time. The bill failed to pass the House February 8, 1978, however, even though it was modified (H.R. 9718) after being reported from the Government Operations Committee in May of 1977. The measure never came up for a vote on the Senate floor although it was reported by the Government Affairs Committee with relative ease on May 16, 1977.

The bill would have established the Agency for Consumer Protection (ACP). This agency would have had the power to intervene in formal adjudicatory or rulemaking proceedings if the agency's administrator felt it was necessary to protect consumer interests. The agency also would have been able to intervene with oral or written arguments in executive branch decisions affecting consumers. In a more controversial section, the ACP would have had the power to initiate judicial review of another agency's proceedings in which the ACP had participated if the proceedings were otherwise reviewable under the law. The compromise House draft dropped another provision which gave the ACP the right to appeal decisions in which it had not been a party. The bill gave the ACP the right to join in legal proceedings initiated by others, but unlike similar measures of earlier years it did not give the right to intervene in state and local proceedings. The bill withheld from ACP the power to intervene in defense and intelligence agencies as well as in labor disputes or agreements. This latter exemption was criticized by some as a political move to gain labor support, but provisions of other laws might have greatly constrained the freedom of the ACP to intervene in this area. The House version also exempted many farm-related programs, although this section was dropped from the Senate bill in the 95th Congress. The Senate version exempted the license renewal proceedings of the FCC and actions the ACP might have taken to restrict the sale or possession of firearms as well as the defense, intelligence, and labor matters covered by the House bill.

The agency also would have had the functions of collecting and evaluating consumer complaints, providing information services, conducting research, holding conferences, and making legislative and policy recommendations to the President. A key provision would have given the ACP the authority to request information from businesses if needed to "protect the health or safety of consumers or to discover consumer fraud or substantial economic injury to consumers" with enforcement power in the U.S. district courts. Trade secrets and small businesses were protected, but after much business opposition this interrogatory power was dropped in the House redraft. Also deleted were provisions allowing ACP to set up regional offices and a consumer product testing lab (rating of products was prohibited in any case). In an effort to keep down first-year costs, the House compromise also required the transfer of all duplicative consumer offices in the government to the ACP.

The bill required federal agencies to inform the ACP of decisions likely to affect consumers, and the redraft required the ACP to inform the White House of its intention to appeal nonregulatory decisions of federal agencies. The Senate version directed federal agencies to issue rules relating to the rights of affected individuals to file complaints, petitions, obtain information or participate in proceedings. It also contained the so-called Brock Amendment from the 1975 version, which required agencies promulgating rules under the Administration Procedures Act to prepare a cost/benefit statement for rules having a substantial economic impact. The House bill contained a sunset provision requiring ACP reauthorization by September 30, 1982, or it would have faced abolition.

Payment of attorney's fees for public participation. The major bills for government payment of reasonable attorney's fees were S. 270, sponsored by Senator Edward M. Kennedy (D-Mass.) and fourteen cosponsors, and H.R. 8798, sponsored by Representative Peter Rodino (D-N.J.) and nineteen cosponsors; they did not fare well in the 95th Congress. The Kennedy bill, which was reported in the 94th Congress by the Senate Judiciary Committee, was defeated in committee on a tie vote. The Senate Government Affairs Committee gave priority to the consumer agency measure and, recognizing the existence of significant opposition, did not try to report the attorney's fee bill. In the House Judiciary Committee, Chairman Rodino took the same attitude toward his bill, H.R. 3361, which was reported out of subcommittee but was sent back to be redrafted (H.R. 8798) after meeting some resistance in the full committee.

Both bills would have authorized the payment of reasonable attorney's fees "at the prevailing market rate" in agency proceedings and in civil cases reviewing agency actions. Under the Kennedy bill, persons would be eligible if their representation of an interest could "reasonably be expected to contribute substantially to a fair determination of the proceeding." Account was to be taken of (1) whether the interest was already adequately represented, (2) the number and complexity of the issues, (3) the importance of encouraging participation by "segments of the population who, as individuals, may have little economic incentive to participate," and (4) the need for a "fair balance of interests." It was stipulated that the person's economic interest in the outcome of the proceeding must be small in comparison with the costs of effective participation, or that the person must lack sufficient resources of his own to participate effectively without government assistance. Fees were not to be paid if the participant acted in an "obdurate, dilatory, mendacious, or oppressive manner." Awards were to be limited to $75 an hour unless the agency found that special factors justified a higher fee. The courts could have awarded attorney's fees if the requesting party received the relief sought "in substantial measure" or if the action served "an important public purpose." The requesting party would have to have passed the same economic means test required in cases of agency awards to participants. The bill authorized appropriations of $10 million for a three-year experiment in public funding of participation.

The redrafted Rodino bill proposed an additional standard for awards in cases of judicial review. It would have restricted payment to cases involving actions related directly to health, safety, civil rights, the environment, or the economic well-being of consumers. Another measure (H.R. 2104), sponsored by Representative John Murphy (D-N.Y.), would have limited awards to participants in proceedings or judicial review of regulations under only three laws: the Flammable Fabrics Act, Federal Hazardous Substances Act, and orders under the National Traffic and Motor Vehicle Safety Act of 1966.

Expansion of rights under class action suits. After a period of expanding the ability of consumers to bring class action suits (those which represent a common interest of a large number of persons) the courts in recent years have begun to limit class action suits that allege financial loss because of price fixing or other injuries due to corporate abuses of law.

These suits are considered important by consumer advocates because the amount of money involved for each member of the class may be too small to give an incentive for individual action. When collective suits are brought, costs can be shared, and the large amount of potential money damages not only provides attorneys with incentives to participate but also deters illegal behavior by potential defendants. On the other hand, businessmen note that the number and cost of class action suits has risen so much in the last decade that the incentives provided for attorneys to bring these suits may be too great, leading to frivolous suits and "fishing expeditions."

Because the courts have recently been more restrictive in interpreting the Federal Rules of Civil Procedure as they apply to class actions, consumerists want to pass new rules that would limit judicial discretion and make it easier to bring this type of suit. One general class action proposal (S. 3475), which was introduced August 25, 1978, was sponsored for the Carter administration by Senator Dennis DeConcini (D-Ariz.), chairman of the Subcommittee on Improvement in Judicial

Machinery, and cosponsored by Senator Kennedy. A number of other general bills concerning class actions have been introduced in the past to deal with the problems such suits have in meeting the minimum damages and cost of notice requirements of Rule 23 of the Federal Rules of Civil Procedure. Recent Supreme Court decisions have ruled that individuals bringing class action suits must (1) meet the dollar minimums set by statute and cannot aggregate the claims of the entire class to reach the minimum, and (2) pay for the cost of informing all members of the class about the suit and inform them individually where possible regardless of the cost.

The class action provisions of the proposed Federal Trade Commission (FTC) Amendments (S. 1288) sponsored by Senator Wendell Ford (D-Ky.) and the original version of H.R. 3816, sponsored by Representative Bob Eckhardt (D-Tex.), would have allowed aggregation of damages to reach the minimum damage figure and would have given the courts wide discretion in selecting methods of giving notice to members of a class (such as through the use of radio, television, or newspapers). Another provision would have allowed the courts wide discretion in selecting methods of establishing damages and thus would have further eased the burdens on those bringing class actions. However, the provisions of the FTC-related class action bills would have applied only in these cases where the FTC had issued a cease-and-desist order to stop a violation of an FTC rule or an unfair or deceptive practice.

The provisions of the administration's class action bill (S. 3475) were not limited to FTC-related offenses. The first section of the bill was devoted to actions involving small claims (under $300 per person and involving 200 or more persons) in which at least one "substantial" question of law or fact was common to the affected parties. The bill would have replaced the traditional class action with a "public action" brought by the United States or on behalf of the United States by one or more injured persons. Because only a single claim would be vested in the United States, there was no requirement to notify members of the class and no need for elaborate procedures to define the class and establish adequate representation. The "substantial" common issue did not have to predominate as it does under current Rule 23 procedures. Once a public judgment against a defendant was handed down, however, no small-claim individual actions were permitted. Instead, injured parties were allowed to file individual claims with the Administrative Office of the United States Courts, which would receive the money from the defendant. The court was to be allowed wide discretion in determining methods of assessing damages, and proof of each individual's injury was not required.

When actions were initiated on behalf of the United States, the government could (1) enter and assume control, (2) allow the action to proceed, (3) designate a state attorney general to take over the case if he so elected, or (4) recommend that the action not be allowed because it was not in the public interest. An incentive to bring public actions was provided by a $10,000 award plus attorney's fees to be awarded to a successful plaintiff and charged to the defendant. Class actions in which the damages were over $300 per person and which involved forty or more persons were to be treated in the traditional class action manner, but there was no requirement of aggregate harm other than that the injury arise out of a substantially common question of law or fact. The court would still have had to determine whether all elements of a class action were met, but the procedures of Rule 23 (b)(3) were simplified. In fact, the bill provided a series of simplified procedures to reduce the time and money costs of both the public and class action suits and to reduce the chances of arbitrary dismissal of both types by unsympathetic judges.

Partly because of the Carter administration's caution in submitting its general class action bill, advocates of expanded class action suits made little progress in the 95th Congress in arriving at an approach to counter the recent court decisions. In one area partially related to class action, however, the Senate Judiciary Committee did act and reported a bill (S. 1874) sponsored by Senator Kennedy with Senators Robert Morgan (D-N.C.) and John Danforth (R-Mo.). Entitled the Antitrust Enforcement Act of 1978, the bill would have reversed the Supreme Court decision in *Illinois Brick Co.* v. *Illinois,* 431 U.S. 720 (1977). This decision held that indirect purchasers (the ultimate consumer) of products that were subject to price fixing could not recover damages. One of the reasons given was that defendants (producers) would then face the possibility of multiple damages for the same injury because direct purchasers (wholesalers) could also sue for damages without having to prove that the extra costs of the price fixing were not passed on to the consumer (the "pass-on" defense). Rather than overrule a previous Court decision and allow the defendants (producers) in such cases the opportunity to use the "pass-on" argument as a defense against suits from direct purchasers, the Court decided that it was more practical to outlaw individual and class action suits from indirect purchasers and let suits from direct purchasers provide the deterrent against price fixing.

A majority of the Senate Judiciary Committee disagreed with this strategy since merchandisers might receive "windfall" legal awards which they would not have to pass on to their customers. The committee majority also felt that the decision was contrary to recent congressional action in a related area of antitrust policy. Several witnesses testified at committee hearings that reducing the incentives for original purchasers to bring private antitrust suits and, instead, allowing indirect purchasers to bring class action suits would result in a net *decrease* in antitrust enforcement and deterrents to price fixing because the incentives for class action are much weaker than for antitrust suits by first purchasers. The committee majority was not swayed by this line of reasoning, however. It argued that first purchasers are reluctant to sue their suppliers because of ongoing business relations and because they have frequently passed on their costs to their customers.

An amendment to S. 1874 attempted to redress the balance toward the concerns of business. It reversed the Supreme Court finding in *Pfizer, Inc.* v. *Government of India,* in which foreign governments were ruled to be "persons" within the meaning of the antitrust laws and thus allowed to sue for treble damages (unlike the U.S. government, which is limited to actions for single damages). However, other business-oriented amendments to S. 1874 were defeated. These included provisions to (1) reduce the chances of duplicative recovery by forcing consolidation of suits from both direct and indirect purchasers; (2) eliminate retroactive application of the proposed law; and (3) limit recovery to three times the original overcharge. Because of strong opposition from business, the bill was never scheduled for a floor vote.

Other Proposals

Eliminating Contradictory and Duplicative Regulations. Many sunset bills aim for the elimination of duplicative and conflicting regulations. In June of 1978, however, Senator Lloyd Bentsen (D-Tex.), with Representative Clarence Brown (R-Ohio) acting as cosponsor, introduced a measure (S. 3263, H.R. 14166) for the specific purpose of ending such regulations. Entitled the Regulatory Conflicts Elimination Act, it required the director of the Office of Management and Budget (OMB) to submit to the President, Congress, and the head of each independent agency an annual report that (1) identified duplicative and conflicting regulations, (2) determined the cost of compliance with these rules, (3) made recommendations for their elimination or modification, and (4) reported on progress toward this goal made by the departments in the previous year. The President would have to develop criteria to measure costs of compliance accurately and to determine which rules were covered by the legislation. By October 1 of each year, the President and the heads of the departments would have to submit to Congress and the comptroller general a report on which rules were to be modified or dropped. Thirty days after receipt of the report, the comptroller general would have to submit to Congress an evaluation of the report of the OMB director and the President's recommendations. Rule changes recommended by the President would take effect automatically unless, within sixty days of receiving the President's recommendations, Congress passed a concurrent resolution disapproving them. The Bentsen proposal was added to the Muskie sunset bill on the floor and was passed by the Senate immediately before adjournment.

Elimination of conflicting rules would seem to be a noncontroversial proposal, but certain groups may have strong vested interests in retaining many of them. For example, after the Occupational Safety and Health Administration (OSHA) targeted 1,100 nitpicking safety rules for elimination, it encountered resistance from parties who wanted to save some of those rules. As another example, there had initially been resistance to Senator Bentsen's amendments to reduce paperwork in two federal programs, the Comprehensive Employment and Training Act (CETA) program (S. 2570, H.R. 12452) and the federal housing mortgage programs (S. 3084). By unanimous approval during floor debate on July 20, 1978, the mortgage-related proposal was added as an amendment to the bill reauthorizing the Federal Housing Program, and it was still in the bill when it became a law (P.L. 95-557). It forced the Federal Housing Administration, the Veterans Administration, and any other federal housing agencies to use the same note and mortgage forms, loan application forms, appraisal forms, and settlement statements. Yet the General Accounting Office (GAO) had been recommending a similar consolidation for fifteen years with the agencies involved consistently opposing it! The senator's other proposal, attached as an amendment to the bill reauthorizing CETA, was adopted unanimously on the floor before passage on August 25 and will help eliminate some of the estimated 100 million man-hours spent annually by the program's prime sponsors on paperwork required by the Labor Department. It also will require the secretary of labor to cut compliance costs imposed by rules governing the program and will require him to report annually to Congress on its progress. The provision was accepted by the conference and became law (P.L. 95-524).

Proposals for Studies and Reports. The House Commerce Subcommittee on Oversight and Investigations and the Senate Government Affairs Committee both undertook and completed comprehensive studies of regulatory reform during 1976 and 1977, and the American Bar Association had its own blue-ribbon commission in 1977. In spite of this, a number of bills were introduced in January 1977 which would have established a blue-ribbon, Hoover-type national commission on regulatory reform, as President Ford had suggested during the 94th Congress. Bills of this type were sponsored by Representatives Silvio Conte (R-Mass., H.R. 284); Kenneth Robinson (R-Va., H.R. 640); Jerry Patterson (D-Calif., H.R. 2616); and Tom Hagedorn (R-Minn., H.R. 2586). A similar provision existed in Senator Edmund Muskie's (D-Me.) sunset bill (S. 2) as it was introduced and later passed by the Senate.

The Interim Regulatory Reform Act (S. 263), sponsored by Senators James Pearson (R-Kan.) and Warren Magnuson (D-Wash.) and passed by the Senate, took a narrower approach. It called for the independent agencies to study their governing statutes and the court decisions on their laws and make recommendations to Congress for recodification and revision of such laws. As already noted, the 1530 series of interim regulatory reform bills called for a similar effort with regard to agency regulations.

Eliminating Delays and Protecting Rights in Agency Proceedings. A number of reforms in agency procedures have been jointly endorsed by the American Bar Association and the Administrative Conference of the United States, including the section of S. 1721 already discussed which would expand public notice and comment in rulemaking proceedings and allow for expedited procedures in rate-making cases if the interests of affected parties are protected. On June 20, 1977, Senator James Abourezk (D-S.D.) introduced a companion bill, S. 1720, which contained three other proposals jointly endorsed by outside legal groups. The first proposal would have extended to informal adjudications and formal rulemaking proceedings the guarantees for strict separation of advocacy and adjudicatory functions and personnel which now apply to formal adjudicatory proceedings. Most agencies already follow such practices, but this proposal would make it official policy to do so. Because of opposition from some agencies that allow top supervisory personnel to attend commission meetings related to cases under their direction, a qualification in the bill allowed supervisory personnel to advise the agency on a case if that official had not personally participated in the investigation or litigation of the case.

The second proposal contained in S. 1720 would have allowed regulatory agencies to delegate final decisions to special review boards rather than causing a logjam at the top by forcing the commissioners to review all cases. Delays caused by such logjams are considered one reason commissioners have less time for general policy setting. The commissioners would retain the right to review any case they considered important or all cases if they so desired. Although this reform would have reduced delay, it made some regulated parties uneasy since they sometimes consider that a final appeal to the commissioners has a better chance of receiving a favorable hearing than one addressed to staff and administrative law judges.

The third proposal in the bill gave all agencies the subpoena power for use in their proceedings. Most agencies that routinely conduct formal proceedings already have such power, but a few agencies such as the Federal Drug Administration and the Department of the Interior have an inadequate grant of the power or none at all. This section did not establish any new investigative powers but simply allowed agencies to resolve major issues of fact in proceedings on the basis of other than voluntarily submitted evidence. Despite joint endorsements from outside legal groups, both S. 1720 and S. 1721 died in subcommittee. This was not surprising, since legislation to reduce administrative delays typically restricts some of the legal opportunities of regulated interests.

After the Senate Government Affairs Committee study of regulation indicated that delay was the most often mentioned complaint about agency decision making, Senator Ribicoff with five cosponsors introduced his own administrative reform bill (S. 2490) in February 1978. Title II contained sections similar to those in S. 1720 to extend separation of function rules to formal rulemaking, to authorize review boards, and to grant the subpoena power to agencies. The bill also had a number of provisions not in Abourezk's Judiciary Committee bill. Title I required each agency to establish an office in charge of planning and management if it did not already have one. At the start of a proceeding this office was to adopt a deadline for completion of the proceeding, and it was to report to Congress each year on its track record for meeting these deadlines and on what it was doing to complete action on those delayed the longest. The report to Congress would also have described regulatory agency priorities each year. The office was also to be responsible for seeing that procedures were expedited as much as possible and that regulations were periodically reviewed. Title II required the use of more informal procedures in certain formal rulemaking cases (such as rate-making and initial license proceedings) and made them optional in other cases now covered by trial-type proceedings. The new procedures would have allowed individuals or parties a chance to submit briefs and present oral arguments on the relevant facts and law. There would have been no formal witnesses and no cross-examination. Formal trial-type hearings could have been held subsequently only if the initial proceedings demonstrated a need for them. Even when such formal hearings were held, expedited procedures could have been used that would rely more on written testimony and eliminate oral testimony and cross-examination. This set of reforms has already been enacted in some laws establishing new regulatory programs. Agencies would also have had to maintain a file of significant actions and prior rulings. It was hoped that this would reduce the amount of legal research attorneys for private parties would need in preparing cases.

Eliminating Anticompetitive Regulations. One of the chief goals of sunset proposals to review all federal programs as well as of specific proposals for the deregulation of regulatory agencies (such as those concerned with airlines and surface transportation) is to eliminate anticompetitive federal regulations. Many people felt at the start of the 95th Congress that a frontal assault on such regulatory programs would be defeated by strong opposition from interest groups which benefit from such programs. Consequently, support arose for an alternative approach that had first been developed in the 93rd Congress. Called the Competitive Improvements Act of 1978 and sponsored by Antitrust and Monopoly Subcommittee Chairman Ted Kennedy, S. 2625 contained language identical to that in a bill which had been reported by the Senate Judiciary Committee in the 94th Congress (S. 2028). The bill's goal had received support from both liberals and conservatives, but conservatives opposed the particular method used to reduce anticompetitive regulations, that of creating a "uniform antitrust standard." In the 95th Congress the bill was not even reported by the Senate Judiciary Committee. The proposed law stated that no federal agency could take any action that would substantially lessen competition, tend to create a monopoly, or maintain a situation burdening competition unless the action could pass the three-part test of the new uniform antitrust standard. To pass the test (1) the actions had to be necessary to accomplish an "overriding statutory purpose" of the agency, (2) the anticompetitive effects had to be clearly outweighed by "significant and demonstrable benefits to the general public," and (3) the objectives could not be accomplished by alternate means with fewer anticompetitive effects.

The attorney general would have had the power to require the agency to hold a hearing if he found an agency not in compliance. Agencies would have had to inform the attorney general of pending actions subject to the antitrust standard, and the attorney general and the Federal Trade Commission would have had the right to participate in any administrative or judicial proceeding involving the antitrust standard. An earlier draft section requiring the publication of antitrust impact statements was dropped from the bill in the 94th Congress.

Although S. 2625 would have created no new rights to judicial review, any action that was reviewable in the courts could have been attacked on the ground that it violated the antitrust standard. The burden of proof would have been on the agency to show that it had complied, and attorney's fees could have been paid to those meeting the means test in S. 270. The version of S. 2625 initially introduced in the 94th Congress granted universal standing for such judicial review of compliance with the antitrust standard and would have required the courts to review agency application of that standard on a *de novo* basis. Both of these sections were dropped in the 95th Congress. However, opponents of the measure still argued that in trying to rid the government of anticompetitive regulation through a judicial strategy and a tough antitrust standard, S. 2625 would have overburdened the courts with suits and caused innumerable delays in agency decision making that would have either disrupted the economy or aided regulated industries in their efforts to prevent change.

Sunset Legislation for Mandatory Review of Programs. Legislation to require review of all or almost all federal programs once every few years was very popular in the 95th Congress. Senator Muskie's S. 2 had over fifty senators as cosponsors, and its House counterpart, H.R. 1756, filed by Representative James Blanchard (D-Mich.) along with other sunset bills, had 140 cosponsors. Many consumer advocates favored the bill because they wanted a review of rate regulation agencies like the Interstate Commerce Commission, while many parties sympathetic to business interests desired a review of safety and social regulation agencies like OSHA, Environmental Protection Agency (EPA), and Equal Employment Opportunity Commission (EEOC). The Muskie bill was designed to appeal to both sides by including all programs and giving individual committees discretion to decide exactly how much emphasis to put on each program. This discretion has been of some concern to those who think the Muskie bill took on too much and would have led to many "rubber stamp" reviews, a diffusion of media attention, and a backlogged Senate schedule. However, opponents of the Muskie approach were unable to come up with a politically viable alternative.

Apart from the problem of scope, the major issue confronting sunset legislation is whether reauthorization should even be part of the sunset process. Given the political pressures created by program beneficiaries, it is thought that the only way to get most authorizing committees to review programs seriously is to create action-forcing mechanisms such as automatic termination (the setting sun) for any program that is not reviewed and reauthorized. Since the sunset concept does not create new political incentives to mobilize the general public against outdated programs, it is no guarantee that needed reforms will occur. Advocates hope, however, that the publicity generated by program critics will help mobilize support for change. At least requiring reauthorizations will put programs reviews on the congressional agenda where the chances of publicity are greatest.

Opponents of automatic termination point out that it is possible to put program reviews on the congressional agenda (as the Ford administration proposal would have in the 94th Congress) without requiring reauthorization. They argue that the key to reform is the presence of a political climate favorable to change in a program area, and the threat of automatic termination has no effect because reviews can be merely *pro forma*. Sunset adversaries are also worried that required reauthorizations will give the President too much power (because of his ability to veto the reauthorizations), create possibilities for terminations which are accidental or unsupported by a majority of the members of Congress, create scheduling inflexibilities for Congress, reduce the chances of cooperation from executive branch agencies, and provide incentives for those subject to federal regulation to delay compliance with rules in hopes the agency will be terminated.

Since the chief proposals in the 95th Congress (S. 2 for nonregulatory programs and the Percy-Byrd-Ribicoff-sponsored S. 600 for regulatory agencies) both contained automatic termination features, the arguments of opponents—especially powerful committee chairmen—had to be defused before the bill could gain enough support for passage. This finally occurred in the Senate in the late summer of 1978, and S. 2 with part of S. 600 added as an amendment was passed by the Senate

29

October 11, 1978. The other Senate sunset bill, S. 1244 filed by Senator Joseph Biden (D-Del.), partially duplicated S. 2 and was not included. It would have limited the period of authorization for budget authority in appropriations acts. In the House, the chairman of the Government Operations Committee with jurisdiction over the sunset bills, Representative Brooks, opposed automatic termination. Consequently, bills which lacked any termination features—for example, H.R. 10421, filed by Butler Derrick (D-S.C.) and thirteen cosponsors—were considered to have the best chance of House passage.

Several other issues confront sunset bills. One is exactly what should be terminated if an action-forcing feature is included. Muskie's bill would have terminated budget authority for the program in question. Other ways to proceed are to terminate the agency administering the program and the authority to enforce rules and regulations stemming from the program (S. 600) or to terminate the underlying law itself.

A second issue is the aforementioned problem of how broad to make sunset coverage. As passed by the Senate, the Muskie bill covered every category except those specifically exempted, such as interest on the national debt, enforcement of civil rights, the judicial system, IRS refunds, and several entitlement programs. The original measure also covered tax expenditures (the so-called "loopholes"), but this was dropped. An attempt to pass a separate sunset bill for tax expenditures, S. 125 (sponsored by Senator John Glenn (D-Ohio), failed. The Percy-Byrd-Ribicoff measure applied to thirty-two major regulatory agencies grouped by subject category. As originally introduced, it exempted from termination those rules the President deemed essential to public health and safety, but this exemption was dropped to bring S. 600 into conformity with S. 2 before they were merged. Some bills covered only a few key regulatory agencies out of a concern about trying to do too much too soon and diffusing media coverage and political support. Two such bills were H.R. 3181, the Regulatory Agency Self-Destruct Act, sponsored by Representative Abner Mikva (D-Ill.), and H.R. 3411, the Federal Agency Pilot Termination and Review Act, sponsored by Representative Lee Hamilton (D-Ind.).

A number of bills (including the initial version of the Muskie bill in the 94th Congress) called for the use of "zero-base" program reviews in the federal government. Since the Carter administration argued that zero-base budgeting was a device best left to the discretion of the executive branch, Muskie changed the name of his sunset bill to Program Reauthorization and Evaluation Act of 1978 and eventually to the Sunset Act of 1978.

A third issue is how long to make the sunset cycle. The Muskie bill originally started with five years and was changed to six years when reported from the Government Affairs Committee. It ended up with a ten-year cycle after a redraft was cleared by the Rules Committee. The Percy-Byrd-Ribicoff bill originally had an eight-year cycle that was also changed to ten years to conform to S. 2.

A fourth matter pertains to which agencies of government to involve in the program reviews. The Muskie bill as passed by the Senate required agencies covered by a review to submit to OMB and the Congress a report covering the eight criteria established for the reviews. OMB would forward comments on the report to

Congress. The S. 600 part of the bill called for an analysis and a legislative plan to be submitted to Congress by the President covering eight areas along with a joint OMB-GAO evaluation of the agencies involved and a later assessment of the President's plan by OMB and GAO.

A fifth and related matter is how detailed to make the instructions to the authorizing committee concerning its program reviews that are required before new budget authority can be considered. Some committee chairmen object to detailed instructions. They are concerned that such an approach would give the parliamentarians of the House and Senate (who answer to the leadership) great power to rule the consideration of new budget authority out of order if they disagreed with the authorizing committee's review. Muskie thus dropped the detailed instructions in favor of relatively vague ones covering four broad areas of concern. A more detailed set of criteria to be used for ''comprehensive reviews'' was changed so that it would only be required to the extent the committee ''deemed necessary.''

A sixth concern is the timing of termination. The Muskie bill cut off all budget authority at once. The original version of S. 600 contained a phased termination of an agency's authority to enforce rules over a six-month period.

A seventh matter, which turned out to be crucial to Senate passage of S. 2, concerns safeguards to extend the deadlines to prevent accidental or unwanted terminations when the original schedule cannot be met. As passed by the Senate, the Muskie bill contained a provision for ''required authorization waiver resolutions'' that would allow enough new budget authority for one year to maintain the level of services currently provided by the agency concerned. The resolutions could be introduced whenever floor debate had proceeded fifteen hours or the President had vetoed a bill. In addition, other safeguards existed since the houses of Congress could change their rules to allow a resolution authorizing new budget authority to be ''in order'' at any time.

As passed, S. 2 called for each government program (except those with explicit exemptions) to be reauthorized at least once every ten years. Bills establishing new budget authority would be out of order unless accompanied by a reauthorization review with recommendations on what parts of the program should be modified, terminated, or left unchanged. To the extent deemed appropriate by the authorizing committee, these reviews would have to cover (1) information on program costs, results, effectiveness, and so forth; (2) identification of conflicting and overlapping programs; (3) program goals and expected results; and (4) a comparison of new budget authority with that for each of the previous four years.

Committees would have to decide which of the programs under their jurisdiction would be selected for ''comprehensive reexamination,'' and they would not be given a funding resolution approving their committee budget unless they had done so and explained their plans in a report. In selecting programs for comprehensive review, they would have to take into account (1) the amount of time that had passed since the program had been in effect; (2) the extent to which the program required change; (3) the resources of the committee; and (4) the desirability of examining related programs concurrently.

The comprehensive program examinations themselves were required—''to the extent the committee deems appropriate''—to deal with eight subjects including program objectives, changing conditions, duplicative and conflicting objectives, number of beneficiaries, assessment of effectiveness, cost/effectiveness and where appropriate a cost/benefit analysis, the merits of alternatives, and impacts of a regulatory, privacy, and paperwork nature. Departments under review would have had to submit their reports six months before the required completion date for the committee reviews.

The part of the bill containing the Percy amendments on regulatory agencies would have had the President submit his analysis of programs up for review on February 1 of the first session, the legislative plan on April 1 of that session, and the joint OMB-GAO evaluation of the plan on June 1 of the same year. The President's analysis would have been required to contain information concerning agency purposes, changed conditions, net agency impact and effectiveness, timeliness of agency decision making, cost-effectiveness, inflation impacts, and practical alternative approaches. The legislative plan would have included recommendations on consolidation and elimination of functions, organizational reforms, merger and abolition of agencies, elimination of conflicting or outdated rules, alleviating delays, increasing public participation, and increasing cost-effectiveness and economic competition. The President would also have had to submit a report on the cumulative impact on specific industry groupings of all government regulatory activity reviewed to that date and recommendations to ensure that the cumulative impact was ''in the nation's best interest.'' The reauthorization review of the congressional committee would have had to compare its recommendations with those of the President and explain the basis for its own findings.

SUBSTANTIVE REFORMS

Reduced Regulation

Airlines. Legislation gradually to eliminate price and route regulation of the nation's airlines was the major deregulatory achievement of the 95th Congress. The President signed into law the Airline Deregulation Act of 1978 (S. 2493) on October 24, 1978 (P.L. 95-504). The issue received its first significant attention when Senator Kennedy, as chairman of the Senate Judiciary Subcommittee on Administration Practice and Procedures, held oversight hearings on the Civil Aeronautics Board in 1975. In 1976, Senator Howard Cannon's (D-Nev.) Commerce Subcommittee on Aviation held hearings on the general topic of aviation regulatory reform. At the start of the 95th Congress, Senators Cannon and Kennedy introduced S. 689 to reduce the Civil Aeronautics Board's powers over rate setting and route licensing. One of the bill's most controversial methods of intensifying competition among the airlines was "automatic market entry," whereby airlines would have been able to obtain a quota of new route authority each year without having to apply for CAB approval. A later redraft (S. 2493) incorporated portions of Senator Pearson's proposal to change the subsidy system for small communities to assure continuation of local service. Senator Pearson had earlier filed his own airline deregulation bill (S. 292).

In the House, Representative Glenn Anderson (D-Calif.), the chairman of the Public Works Subcommittee on Aviation, introduced with five cosponsors H.R. 8813 and later H.R. 11145. The latter was a compromise measure that attempted to resolve the controversy over automatic market entry. Representative Elliott Levitas (D-Ga.) introduced a more modest deregulation bill (H.R. 9297), which was the first to include a sunset provision for abolishing the CAB (in 1983) but which also mandated very cautious graduation in reducing CAB regulation.

As enacted into law, the Airline Deregulation Act permits carriers to lower air fares by as much as 50 percent below or raise them 5 percent above the "standard industry fare" (the fare as of July 1, 1977) without prior CAB approval. New operating rights are to be granted to any carrier requesting to serve a route on which only one other carrier is actually providing service. Automatic market entry without prior CAB approval is authorized for each airline on one additional route each year during the 1979–1981 period. At the same time, each airline is allowed to protect one of its existing routes each year from automatic entry.

The legislated "declaration of policy" (which provides overall guidance to the CAB) was also changed to place "maximum reliance" on competition. Service to many smaller communities was left open by a provision authorizing the CAB to order a carrier to maintain "essential air transportation service" and for the CAB to continue for a ten-year period to provide subsidies or seek other carriers to assure this service. The interests of airline employees were protected by making employees who had worked for carriers for four years eligible for compensation for up to six years if they were hurt economically by the new competition policies. Small commuter airlines were exempted from CAB regulation, and the rights of charter airlines were protected.

The ability of the President to disapprove international route awards was also restricted. Perhaps most important, the CAB's authority over domestic routes would cease at the end of 1981; its authority over domestic fares would end at the end of 1982, and the board would be abolished at the end of 1984 unless Congress acted to extend those dates.

Partial air cargo deregulation, originally part of the Anderson bill in the House, was relatively noncontroversial. For this reason it was taken out of the Anderson bill and attached to another measure, H.R. 6010 by Representatives Anderson and Gene Snyder (R-Ky.), that contained other miscellaneous changes of a noncontroversial nature. To carriers already handling cargo exclusively the bill gave certificates to operate throughout the country, while other airlines could apply for all-cargo certification one year after enactment. The bill also removed most CAB controls on cargo rates and routes flown. The measure was signed into law November 9, 1977 (P.L. 95-163).

Communications. Congress took its first tentative steps toward partial deregulation and increased competition in the communications field in June 1978 when Representative Lionel Van Deerlin (D-Calif.), chairman of the House Commerce Subcommittee on Communications, and ranking minority member Louis Frey, Jr. (R-Fla.) jointly introduced the Communications Act of 1978 (H.R. 13015) after twenty months of hearings and investigations. An indication of the direction the subcommittee was headed was its neglect of H.R. 8, the Consumer Communication Reform Act, a bill introduced by Representative Teno Roncalio (D-Wyo.) at the request of AT&T to restrict the degree of competition in telephone communications.

The Van Deerlin-Frey bill would have changed the declaration of policy of the Federal Communications Commission (FCC) to restrict federal regulation to those areas where market forces were deficient. Radio broadcasting would have been deregulated except for technical matters with licenses granted indefinitely unless their holders violated the law. Television licensing regulation would also have been relaxed although to a lesser degree. Television licenses would have been granted for five years instead of three and, after ten years, they too would have been granted indefinitely. Regulation of television program content would have been relaxed. Political candidates would still have had to receive equal opportunities on television, but this would not have applied to the contest for any statewide or national office. Television stations would have had to carry news and public affairs programs and treat controversial issues only "in an equitable manner" (instead of using the current "fairness doctrine"). Moreover, the new commission would *not* have had to establish procedures to ascertain the "problem, needs and interests of a service area."

New television stations would have been allocated by "random selection." Radio and television stations would have had to pay spectrum fees based on the value of the spectrum they used. The income from the fees would have been used to fund public broadcasting, minority ownership of stations, and the budget of the new five-person Communications Regulatory Commission, which would have replaced the FCC. Regulation of cable television would have been left to the states. The Corporation for Public Broadcasting would have been replaced with a Public Telecommunicators Programming Endowment whose sole job would have been to provide program grants.

In the telephone field, common carriers would have had three years to divest themselves of equipment manufacturing facilities, but in turn they would have been allowed to enter any other field of telecommunication including cable TV, radio, television, or, most important of all from AT&T's perspective, the computer field in which AT&T has sophisticated equipment which it has been unable to market because of the 1956 antitrust consent decree it signed with the Justice Department. On the other side of the coin, every common carrier would have been required to hook up with every other common carrier unless the commission found that this would result in "substantial technical or economic harm to carriers from whom the connection is sought" and "the harm to the carrier exceeded the benefits to the public that would be created by the connection."

This latter section and the section on cable television were inspired by recent court decisions that criticized the FCC for attempting to protect already established carriers against new forms of competition. So far, the first draft of the bill has been received with cautious optimism by industry sources in the broadcast field, although public interest groups are concerned about the lack of a substantive public interest standard for broadcasters, and broadcasters are not enthusiastic about the deregulation of cable television.

Trucking and Surface Transportation. Little progress was made toward deregulation of surface transportation in the 95th Congress, in part because the Carter administration decided to postpone submission of a trucking deregulation bill pending the outcome of the airline deregulation process. However, a number of bills dealt with two sets of problems: the procedures of the Interstate Commerce Commission (ICC) and the inefficiencies in the trucking system stemming from prohibitions against back-hauling. Under these restrictions truckers who carry unregulated merchandise (such as unprocessed agricultural goods or their own corporation's products) must return home empty. S. 2374 sponsored upon request by Senator Magnuson with three cosponsors contained a number of provisions to expedite ICC procedures and reduce delay. Senator Pearson's bill (S. 547) would have extended to other forms of surface transportation the procedures applicable to railroads. Another measure cosponsored by Magnuson and Pearson, S. 2269, would have exempted common carriers, contract carriers, and freight forwarders from the provisions of the ICC Act that served little or no "useful purpose." Representative Jack Kemp (R-N.Y.) introduced H.R. 2443, which was even more explicit in trying to solve the back-hauling problem. It simply exempted independent owner-operators from ICC regulation, but prohibited them from collecting fees lower than those specified in the ICC tariffs. On a separate front Senator Clifford Hansen (R-Wyo.) proposed a bill (S. 2307) to prohibit household movers from charging an amount that exceeded by more than 10 percent the estimate provided the customer.

Now that their profits are down, some railroads have made it clear in the last few months that they favor more deregulation and procedural reform than was achieved in 1976 railroad reform legislation. It is possible that there will be a renewed interest in railroad regulatory reform in the 96th Congress. In the trucking field, however, the politics are more complicated since the large regulated truckers employ unionized teamsters who, like their employers, do not want to see restrictions lifted on nonunionized independents. Since the public cannot relate easily to the issues involved in surface transportation regulation (unlike airline regulation where the public is a direct consumer of services), it may be difficult to generate popular support.

Others. *Endangered Species Act.* In October 1978, spurred on by a recent Supreme Court decision which stated that the Endangered Species Act's protection of the snail darter prevents completion of TVA's Tellico dam on the Little Tennessee River, Congress passed a change in the Endangered Species Act (S. 2899), introduced by Senator John Culver (D-Iowa) and five cosponsors, which will create a cabinet-level board to decide whether federal projects should be exempted from the law when the benefits of the project clearly outweigh the value of the threatened species (P.L. 95-632). The composition of the board in the final draft was slightly less favorable to environmentalists than an earlier draft.

Saccharin ban delay and nitrite prohibitions. At the end of the first session of the 95th Congress the President signed S. 1750 (P.L. 95-203) sponsored by Senator Kennedy to prohibit the secretary of health, education, and welfare from banning saccharin for eighteen months while HEW arranged for a National Academy of Sciences study on the health effects of the artificial sweetener and other HEW studies of cost/benefit issues. Disclosure provisions were included to inform persons of potential dangers.

About twenty other bills, such as H.R. 11327 (Rep. Tom Hagedorn, R-Minn. and twenty-four cosponsors), were introduced in Congress to prohibit a similar ban on nitrites used in meat until further studies could be conducted or until such time as a substitute preventative for botulism was available. No action was taken on these measures.

Pesticide registration reform. Senator Patrick Leahy (D-N.H.) introduced a bill, S. 1678, to reform the procedures used in the registration of pesticides. It was signed into law September 30, 1978 (P.L. 95-396). The need for this bill was brought out by complaints of farmers that the slowness of the registration process was reducing the availability of effective pesticides and by complaints of small pesticide manufacturers that the procedural costs of registering a new pesticide were prohibitively expensive. New procedures were designed to help alleviate both of these problems. Another provision gave inventors of new pesticides ten years of exclusive use of their safety data and an additional five years of compensation from those who use the data.

Mandatory retirement protection. H.R. 5383 expanded protection of the 1967 Age Discrimination in Employment Act to those between the ages of sixty-five and seventy (P.L. 95-256). Top executives and tenured university faculty members were exempted from the new federal protection, the latter until 1982. The law also removed the seventy-year-old mandatory retirement age for federal employees.

Unsuccessful efforts to reduce regulation. S. 2055, sponsored by Sen. Thomas McIntyre (D-N.H.), would have allowed "negotiable order of withdrawal" accounts (NOW accounts), which are similar to checking accounts that earn interest at all federally chartered or insured institutions. The bill was never scheduled for floor action although reported. However, a provision of the omnibus banking regulation bill (P.L. 95-630) did allow such accounts in New York. Abraham Kazen, Jr.'s (D-Tex.) revision of the bill to make technical improvements in the strip mining control law (H.R. 13553) would have allowed companies with federal coal leases to exchange them *solely* because the land could not be reclaimed. It died in committee.

H.R. 11445, sponsored by Neal Smith (D-Iowa), would have banned the assessment of fines by OSHA for the first ten inspection violations if they were not serious and exempted small businesses from some paperwork requests. It was vetoed by the President.

Nuclear power plant licensing reforms (S. 2775, H.R. 11704) sponsored by Senators Gary Hart (D-Colo.) and Morris Udall (D-Ariz.) would have allowed the Nuclear Regulatory Commission (NRC) to approve sites for nuclear plants prior to filing a construction permit and authorized NRC to approve standard nuclear power plant designs prior to filing of a construction permit. They would also have allowed for joint granting of operating licenses and construction permits. The bills died in committee, but S. 2584, the authorization bill for NRC, required NRC to prepare a report on ways states might participate in siting, licensing, and waste disposal issues.

S. 1503, sponsored by Strom Thurmond (R-S.C.), would have allowed reimbursement for the losses of manufacturers of Tris-treated clothes. The losses resulted when the government required that children's clothes be treated with a flame-retardant chemical and later made them repurchase such clothes because of a cancer danger from the chemical. The bill was vetoed by the President.

Increasing Regulation

Bills That Passed. *Increased banking regulation (H.R. 14279, P.L. 95-630).* In an effort to prevent abuses by bank insiders which came to light during the Bert Lance investigation and to provide increased controls over so-called problem banks (some of which have failed in the last few years), Congress enacted an omnibus banking regulation bill. It set up several restrictions on dealings with bank insiders, including limits on the amount of loans they could be given and prohibitions on preferential loans and overdrafts by bank directors and executives. It also set up mandatory reporting requirements on the loans bank officers received from other banks. Prohibitions against interlocking directorates among both depository and non-depository financial institutions were extended, with the banking community given ten years to comply. To further control "problem banks," bank regulators were given increased authority to (1) impose civil penalties; (2) issue cease-and-desist orders against individual bank officers, as well as the institutions; (3) order dismissal of bank executives for threatening the security of the bank, not just for dishonesty; and (4) require bank holding companies to divest themselves of holdings that threatened the safety of the bank. Federal bank officials were also given authority to reject bank acquisitions by individuals, all of whom would have to give sixty days notice of the proposed acquisition. Another section provided for consumer safeguards in electronic banking transfers (originally a separate bill, H.R. 13007, S. 3156) and a liability limitation on unauthorized electronic transfers. Other consumer-oriented provisions protected the rights of individuals whose bank records were subpoenaed, gave New York banks permission to offer NOW accounts (checking accounts which earn interest), and the interest differential between banks and savings-and-loan associations was eliminated for transaction accounts. Regulation Q, which allows federal authorities to set the maximum interest rates banks can pay, was also extended for two years. The Senate version of the bill, S. 3499, was introduced by Senators Thomas McIntyre (D-N.H.) and Edward Brooke (R-Mass.).

Curbs on overseas corporate payments (S. 305, P.L. 95-213). Spurred by the Watergate-related disclosures of the Securities and Exchange Commission, this legislation, sponsored by William Proxmire (D-Wis.) and Harrison Williams (D-N.J.) in the Senate and Bob Eckhardt (D-Tex.) in the House (H.R. 3815), prohibited American firms from making payments to foreign officials or politicians in an effort to win business contracts from other governments or to influence their legislation or regulations. It provided penalties of up to $1 million for knowing and willful violations by corporations and a $10,000 fine and/or five years in jail for violations by individuals of the firm. It required firms to establish records to account "in reasonable detail" for cash disbursements. An unrelated provision expanded disclosure requirements for investors in equity securities by requiring public identification of the actual purchases of more than 5 percent of a corporation's stock. Previously these could have been listed in street names, which protected the identification of the real owners.

Strip mining controls (H.R. 2, P.L. 95-87). The bill, sponsored by Morris Udall (D-Ariz.) and seventeen cosponsors in the House and by Lee Metcalf (D-Mont.) and four cosponsors in the Senate (S. 7), set performance standards for environmental protection to be met at all major surface mining operations. It provided for joint responsibility and enforcement by the states and the federal government. It also established a self-supporting Abandoned Mine Reclamation Fund to (among other things) restore lands harmed by uncontrolled mining in the past. Finally, it protected certain lands regarded as unsuitable for surface mining.

Nuclear export controls (H.R. 8638, P.L. 95-242). This measure, sponsored by Jonathan Bingham (D-N.Y.) and eight cosponsors in the House and Charles Percy and four cosponsors in the Senate (S. 897), set up new controls on the export of nuclear fuels in an effort to prevent terrorists, unstable political leaders, or conventional governments from diverting these fuels to the production of nuclear weapons without "timely warning." Since some of the newer nuclear plants and fuel production processes popular in the developing nations do not meet the timely warning criterion, the law directs that the United States try to help create an international nuclear fuel bank so that such nations will not need to process the fuel themselves. The Nuclear Regulatory Commission is also authorized to set up standards for the physical safeguard of nuclear fuel. The export standards in the bill are much stricter than those set up at an international conference of nuclear suppliers in January 1978. Opponents of the bill argued that the effects of the legislation would be to harm the U.S. nuclear industry needlessly, since purchasers could go elsewhere to get nuclear fuel without having to put up with the delays that have recently plagued U.S. regulatory control of nuclear exports.

Outer continental shelf leasing (S. 9, P.L. 95-372). The bill will increase environmental controls on outer continental shelf drilling and production. It will also provide for more state participation in leasing off-shore tracts. Finally, it makes changes to foster competition for leases by authorizing use of bidding systems other than the cash-bonus type. The measure was sponsored by Henry Jackson (D-Wash.) and Lee Metcalf (D-Mont.) in the Senate and by John Murphy (D-N.Y.) in the House (H.R. 1614).

Ocean dumping (H.R. 4297, P.L. 95-153). The law, sponsored by Robert Leggett (D-Calif.) and three cosponsors in the House and in different versions by Warren Magnuson and James Pearson (S. 1425) and Jennings Randolph (S. 1527) in the Senate, amended the Marine Protection Act of 1972 to prohibit ocean dumping of leftovers from municipal sewage treatment plants (which may reasonably degrade human welfare or the marine environment) beyond the deadlines already imposed, regardless of the reasons why cities wanted extensions.

Tanker safety (S. 682, P.L. 95-474). Prompted by the 1976 sinking of the tanker *Argo Merchant,* this bill, introduced by Senator Magnuson, required tankers and other ships using U.S. ports to carry electronic collision-prevention equipment, up-to-date charts, and at least one English-speaking deck officer. Ships were forbidden to discharge oily water into the ocean during cleaning operations. Segregated ballasts for oil and water were also required (with retrofitting necessary on bigger ships), but a section to require double hulls on tankers was dropped. Vessels with histories of accidents were prohibited from entering U.S. waters and the government was authorized to use harbor vessel control systems.

Uranium mill waste disposal (H.R. 13650, P.L. 95-604). This bill was aimed at a gap in existing law which leaves no federal agency with explicit authority to regulate or dispose of wastes or "tailings" at abandoned uranium mills. This gap became a concern when cancer rates increased in western U.S. areas where the tailings were used in building construction. The bill requires the Nuclear Regulatory Commission and Environmental Protection Agency to develop standards for disposal of the wastes. The law also directed the Energy Department to enter into agreements with the states to clear up twenty-two abandoned disposal sites. It provided that the U.S. government would pay 90 percent of disposal costs. The attorney general was directed to study whether private firms still operating uranium waste disposal sites could be held liable for damages caused by the wastes.

Foreign bank regulation (H.R. 10899, P.L. 95-369). Since U.S. branches of foreign banks were not subject to federal regulation, they held certain competitive advantages over U.S. banks. In an effort to eliminate these advantages and bring the rapidly growing foreign bank operations under federal control, Congress passed a law extending certain regulations to these institutions including mandatory insurance of deposits, Federal Reserve Board reserve requirements, and restrictions on nonbanking activity. The initial bill was introduced by Fernand St Germain (D-R.I.).

Mine safety regulation (S. 717, P.L. 95-164). This bill, introduced by Harrison Williams (D-N.J.) and twenty-five cosponsors in the Senate and in the House as H.R. 4287 by Joseph Gaydos (D-Pa.) and John Dent (D-Pa.), transferred the authority over mine safety from the Interior Department to the Labor Department, a move long sought by miners. In addition, it extended the provisions of the coal mining law of 1969 to all mines, including those that deal in metals, while repealing the less strict provisions of the law which previously regulated safety in these mines. Finally, it strengthened the coal mine safety law in several ways, establishing expedited procedures for issuing new standards and reviewing old ones, requiring more unannounced inspections, toughening standards on toxic substances, and requiring mandatory closing of mines where there is imminent danger or a "pattern of violations." Mandatory penalties were also set for violations of the law.

Regulation of off-track betting (S. 1185, P.L. 95-515). In a compromise between the interests of race tracks that oppose off-track betting (OTB) and states with a financial stake in OTB, Congress passed a law to allow OTB under certain circumstances rather than ban it altogether, as it almost did at the end of the 94th Congress. Race tracks have complained of lower receipts as a result of OTB systems, which are often located in neighboring states. The new law allows OTB in one state on races in another state if OTB is approved according to a complicated set of conditions. The bill also prohibited a state from taking a larger share of interstate OTB receipts than the state where the race is run. The measure was introduced by Sen. Warren Magnuson (D-Wash.) and nine cosponsors.

Debt collection practices (H.R. 5294, P.L. 95-109). The purpose of this law was to cut down on the harassment of debtors by some of the nation's 4,500 debt collection agencies. Commercial institutions that collect their own debts were excluded from coverage. State laws already covered many of the collection agencies, but thirteen states had no law at all and interstate phone calling by agencies complicated enforcement. Among the actions prohibited were phone calls at unusual or inconvenient times, contact of debtors at their place of employment, third-party contacts that were not court approved (subject to limited exceptions), contacts with the debtor after he or she absolutely refused to pay, harassing tactics, misleading representation, and legal action initiated outside the debtor's local jurisdiction. States with laws similar to the federal one were exempted. The bill was initially introduced by Frank Annunzio (D-Ill.) and nine cosponsors.

Cable television utility pole hook-up (H.R. 7442, P.L. 95-234). This legislation stems from the fact that, because many areas will not allow cable firms to put up their own poles, many cable television companies are dependent on existing utility firms for utility-pole attachments. Since public utilities in several states requested large increases in charges for hook-up, cable firms complained to Congress. The result was a law that authorized the FCC to regulate the rates, terms, and conditions of cable TV attachments to utility poles where these hook-ups are not already regulated by the states. States that have such regulations must certify that they take the interests of cable subscribers into account as well as the utilities' interests in approving rates. The price the cable industry had to pay for this law was another provision of the statute which subjects them to civil penalties for violation of FCC rules from which they had previously been exempt. The measure was initially introduced by Timothy Wirth (D-Colo.) with sixteen cosponsors.

Cellulose home insulation standards (S. 2401, P.L. 95-319). Since Congress was unhappy with the slowness of the Consumer Product Safety Commission in issuing flammability and corrosion standards for cellulose home insulation, which constitutes almost half of the rapidly expanding home insulation market, it enacted an interim set of standards identical to that used by the General Services Administration for federal procurement. The measure was introduced by Senator Wendell Ford (D-Ky.).

Gas station dealers' day in court (H.R. 130, P.L. 95-297). The main purpose of this measure was to protect gas station dealers from arbitrary cancellation of their franchises. The franchiser will be allowed to terminate an agreement if he meets standards of reasonableness defined in the law. Ninety days' notice of termination is required unless reasonableness can be demonstrated. If the termination were based on the franchiser's decision to stop marketing gas in a given geographic area, 180 days' notice is necessary. The retailer is permitted to bring a civil suit in federal court. A separate title requires retailers to post octane ratings for the gas they sell. A third title requires the Energy Department to conduct a study of the oil producers' practice of subsidizing gas stations which they own and report the results to the Congress within eighteen months. This provision replaced one which would have outlawed subsidization without further investigation. However, the President was given authority to take interim actions to prevent any predatory policies subject to congressional approval.

Ban on gun control regulation (H.R. 12930, P.L. 95-429). The efforts of the Treasury Department's Bureau of Alcohol, Tobacco, and Firearms to issue proposed regulations to speed identification of guns used in crimes were blocked when the House approved a section of a Treasury appropriations bill which prohibited the bureau from spending any money to enforce the regulations and cut out $4.2 million from the agency's appropriation. The Senate concurred in the House move. The proposed regulations would have required that all guns manufactured in the United States have unique serial numbers, that gun thefts be reported by dealers within twenty-four hours, and that manufacturers and dealers report quarterly on sales without listing the names of individual purchasers.

Rabbit meat inspection (H.R. 2521). President Carter vetoed this bill to require federal inspection of domestic rabbit meat and spot checks of imported rabbit meat. The President argued that voluntary submission of such meat to federal inspectors had not disclosed any problems. The bill was considered to be of primary interest to large rabbit meat processors who would not have had to reimburse the government for inspections and grading if they were mandatory.

Restrictions on lifting of beef import quotas (H.R. 11545). A bill which would have revised the 1964 Meat Import Act to change the formula under which imported meat is allowed into the country and greatly restricted the President's ability to lift the quotas was passed by the House and sent to the President just before adjournment. The President vetoed it as inflationary. The bill did allow a so-called countercyclical formula to determine imports, whereby more foreign beef would be allowed in the country when beef prices were high and domestic production was low, contrary to the present system. The bill was sponsored by Robert Poage (D-Tex.).

Penalties for illegal shipping rebates (H.R. 9518, S. 2008). Since Sea-Land Services, Inc., admitted to the SEC in 1976 that massive illegal rebating of money from posted tariffs existed in the shipping industry, legislation has been pending to increase penalties for such rebates and expedite enforcement. Under the terms of the bill passed by Congress (H.R. 9518) and vetoed by the President, the Federal Maritime Commission would have been able to impose heavier fines than under present law and suspend the tariff of those firms which ignored a subpoena issued as part of an investigation of rebating practices. The President would have been able to overrule the suspension if it were a case of national interest. The State Department lobbied against the bill because of its potential effects on our trading partners. The President vetoed the bill because the White House has not completed its own review of federal maritime policy. The measure had been originally introduced in the House by John Murphy (D-N.Y.) and five cosponsors and in the Senate by Lee Metcalf (D-Mont.).

Bills That Did Not Pass. *Labor law revision (H.R. 8410, S. 2467).* This legislation, introduced in the House by Frank Thompson (D-N.J.) and in the Senate by Harrison Williams (D-N.J.), was billed as labor's answer to the problem of employers who have refused to bargain with unions regardless of the outcome of representation elections. It passed the House but died in the Senate when attempts to end a filibuster failed. The proposal would have increased penalties for firms which refused to bargain, denying them government contracts and allowing double back pay for employees fired because of union organizing. The filing of court injunctions to compel reinstatement of employees illegally dismissed during organizing activities was also authorized. Also, the National Labor Relations Board would have been allowed to compensate workers for wages they would have received had a contract been negotiated when a firm unlawfully refused to negotiate a first contract. Under the so-called equal access provision, union organizers would have had access to company property on company time to counter arguments made in the workplace by the employer against the union. The bill also set up shorter time deadlines for the holding of union representation elections. Finally, the NLRB would have been expanded from five to seven members.

Common-site picketing (H.R. 4250). By a vote of 217 to 205 the House rejected a proposal long sought by labor unions in the construction industry which would have allowed unions with a grievance against one contractor to picket and close down an entire construction site. In 1951 the Supreme Court had ruled that such actions were illegal secondary boycotts. Both houses had passed such a bill in the 94th Congress, but it was vetoed by President Ford. At the time of the House vote in 1977 the Senate had not yet taken up the matter. The bill was sponsored by Frank Thompson (D-N.J.) in the House.

Oil tanker cargo preference (H.R. 1037). This measure introduced by John Murphy (D-N.Y.) would have required that 9.5 percent of American oil imports be carried in American built and operated tankers. It was strongly backed by the maritime unions but failed in a vote on the House floor. The Senate had not yet considered its bill. American ships are more expensive to build and maintain, so the measure could have led to price increases. For this reason alone, it met strong opposition. The political campaign contributions of the maritime unions became an issue in the debate, but the advisability of setting such a precedent in the cargo field was also a strong factor in the discussions.

No-fault auto insurance standards (S. 1381, H.R. 13048). This measure, sponsored by Warren Magnuson with five cosponsors in the Senate and Bob Eckhardt and twenty-four cosponsors in the House, would have established federal standards for state no-fault automobile insurance systems. Under such a system, the accident victim loses his right to sue other parties unless his damages and injuries are above a certain dollar figure representing basic no-fault coverage, but recovery could still be obtained for pain and suffering, significant and permanent loss of function, and so forth. In return, he is paid for accident losses by his own insurance company, thus reducing legal expenses and theoretically increasing the percentage of each premium dollar that is paid to the victim. According to the bill, states failing to institute a no-fault system meeting the standards within three years would be subjected to a no-fault system administered by the Department of Transportation. The Carter administration backed the bill, while the trial lawyers' lobbying groups intensely opposed it. Opponents argued that the state standards required in the bill were too high and that insurance rates would not be reduced as advocates suggested. Similar legislation passed the Senate in 1974, but no House committee has ever reported it. The bill made it out of subcommittee this year but lost in a vote by the full House Interstate and Foreign Commerce Committee.

Hospital cost containment (H.R. 6575, S. 1391). The Carter administration bill to limit hospital costs relied principally on two mechanisms. First, it required limits on hospital revenue increases each year (set at roughly 9 percent the first year and decreasing each year). Second, it set limitations on major new capital expenditures for hospital construction and equipment at $2.5 billion per year. The limit would be apportioned among the states according to population, with regions with excess beds not allowed any new ones at all. The measure contained a wage "pass-through" provision designed to exclude the wages of nonsupervisory hospital employees from the effect of the controls. The limit on revenues was bitterly fought by health interests, which felt it did not allow for local factors. A compromise measure was proposed allowing for stand-by federal authority in case voluntary efforts to reduce costs failed to achieve specified goals. Just before adjournment, a version of this compromise was attached to a Senate measure (S. 1470), sponsored by Herman Talmadge (D-Ga.), to change the way Medicare and Medicaid bills were paid; it was approved on a floor vote. However, the House took no action on the latter bill after Senate approval. Hospital cost containment as initially intro-duced was sponsored by Paul Rogers (D-Fla.) and Dan Rostenkowski (D-Ill.) in the House and Edward Kennedy (D-Mass.), William Hathaway (D-Me.) and Wendell Anderson (D-Minn.) in the Senate.

In a related action the Senate attached to the bill reauthorizing the nation's health planning system (S. 2410), sponsored by Ted Kennedy, an amendment which required that anyone buying expensive medical equipment get a state-approved "certificate of need." The House rejected a somewhat different move to force closure of underused health facilities when such a provision was dropped from the House version of the health planning bill. However, the reauthorization (which did have some positive incentives for facility closings) still failed to pass the House under suspension of the rules, and the program of health planning was sustained for one year under an omnibus continuing resolution for programs that were not reauthorized before adjournment.

DNA research controls (H.R. 11192, Amdt. 1713 to S. 1217). With some environmentalists arguing that DNA researchers could accidentally create new and untreatable diseases and with some research facilities favoring federal preemption of local restrictions on DNA research, Congress considered setting standards to control DNA-related activities. The National Institutes of Health (NIH) has its own standard, but it does not cover all research institutions. The interim bill considered in the House [sponsored by Harley Staggers (D-W.Va.) and Paul Rogers (D-Fla.)] would have extended the NIH standard to all laboratories for two years and provided penalties for violations. When Senator Kennedy shelved his version of the bill, the momentum for passage disappeared and the measure died.

Accounting profession self-regulation (H.R. 13175). This measure, introduced by Representative John Moss (D-Calif.), would have imposed a mandatory scheme of self-regulation on accounting firms to be overseen by a new National Organiza-tion of Securities and Exchange Commission Accountancy, which in turn would have been answerable to the Securities and Exchange Commission. Pressure for such a program developed in the 1970s after disclosure of illegal and questionable practices by some accounting firms handling companies in financial trouble or involved in making overseas payments. Senator Lee Metcalf's Senate Government Operations Subcommittee on Reports, Accounting, and Management had issued a report in 1977 criticizing accounting firm practices. However, support for mandatory self-regulation dwindled when the SEC failed to endorse any proposals and Representative Moss announced his retirement.

Automatic telephone dialing machine rules (H.R. 9505, S. 2193). Following public reaction against increasing use of automatic telephone dialing machines that do not allow the receiver of the call to disconnect immediately, legislation with over eighty-five cosponsors in the House was introduced to control the use of the machines. The bills would have allowed phone customers the opportunity at least once a year to inform the phone company if they wanted their numbers on the list of those that would not be allowed to receive ''junk'' calls. Such calls would also have been limited to one minute. Fines were provided for violators, but charities and polling and political organizations were exempted from the controls. The chief bills, sponsored by Representative Les Aspin (D-Wis.) and Senator Wendell Anderson (D-Minn.), died in committee.

Clinical lab standards (S. 705). Because of complaints of high error rates in work done by clinical medical laboratories, a bill sponsored by Senator Jacob Javits was introduced to strengthen federal controls over such labs. The measure would have provided for licensing of the clinical facilities and would have imposed quality control and personnel standards. The bill passed the Senate on a voice vote July 28, 1977, but died in the Health Subcommittee in the House.

Liquefied natural gas controls (H.R. 11622, S. 1895). The House approved a measure, sponsored by John Dingell (D-Mich.) and Edward Markey (D-Mass.), to require tough new controls on the storage and transport of liquefied natural gas (LNG) and then attached it to a Senate bill dealing with regular gas pipelines (S. 1895). The House then approved the latter and sent it to conference. However, the Senate did not concur in the LNG amendments since it had not held hearings on its LNG bill sponsored by Senators Wendell Ford (D-Ky.) and James Pearson (R-Kans.). Hence, the bill died. The LNG law would have authorized the secretary of transportation to require operators of pipelines to remove conditions determined to be hazardous; detailed the criteria of what constituted a hazard; required pipeline operators to report on the physical characteristics of their facilities according to rules set by DOT, and allowed exemptions from the reporting requirements in cases of financial burden. Other provisions required leaks to be reported and interim federal safety standards to be set. A different title of the bill authorized the DOT secretary to set standards on location, design, construction, and operation of storage facilities. Criminal penalties were set up for anyone who tried to destroy a pipeline facility.

Seabed mining approval (H.R. 3350, S. 2053). In the continuing absence of an international agreement concerning seabed mining rights, the House and the Senate reported legislation to authorize such mining by U.S. firms. Different versions of the Senate bill were reported by various committees, which did not have an opportunity to resolve their differences, so the bill died before Senate passage. As passed by the House, the bill, sponsored by John Murphy (D-N.Y.) and John Breaux (D-La.), would have authorized the secretary of commerce to license seabed mining operations after determining that they did not interfere with other countries' freedoms of the high seas, conflict with international obligations, or threaten the environment. Economic factors had to be considered in the decisions concerning the environment.

Both Decreasing and Increasing Regulation

The Energy Program. *Natural gas deregulation.* The bill to deregulate natural gas, the Natural Gas Policy Act of 1978 (H.R. 5289, P.L. 95-621), is a partial victory for deregulation but a short-run victory for increased regulation since it subjected some intrastate gas to federal price controls for the first time and imposed many other controls that interfere with the marketplace, despite deregulation of some natural gas sources in 1985. The bill established maximum price ceilings for several categories of intrastate and interstate natural gas which will be adjusted for inflation. The price of newly discovered natural gas will be allowed to rise about 10 percent a year until 1985 when the price controls will be lifted. Either the President, with congressional approval, or Congress itself may reimpose price controls on this gas for an eighteen-month period. Reimposition of price controls could not take effect earlier than July 1, 1985, or later than June 30, 1987. Price controls would remain on some categories of natural gas indefinitely. A system of incremental pricing would be used so that commercial users would pay the brunt of higher costs of new gas at first. During times of emergency the President would have the power to allocate natural gas supplies to high priority users by authorizing distributors to make emergency purchases or by allocating supplies as necessary.

Coal conversion. In addition to the natural gas bill, the omnibus National Energy Act was composed of four other specific acts of Congress. The so-called coal conversion bill, the Power Plant and Industrial Fuel Use Act of 1978 (H.R. 5146, P.L. 95-620), expanded the coal conversion program begun under the Energy Supply and Environmental Coordination Act of 1974. With some exemptions allowed by the secretary of energy for site limitations or environmental or fuel availability reasons, all new electric utility and industrial facilities must use coal or some other alternative to fuel oil or natural gas. Although the Carter administration asked for it, the act did not give the DOE secretary the authority to dictate which alternative fuel will be used. Existing power plants will continue to be subject to orders from DOE to switch to coal either individually or by category with some exemptions allowed for the same reasons as apply to new facilities. In addition, existing facilities are required to use no greater proportion of natural gas in the future than they did in the 1974–1976 period and oil to gas switches are prohibited. After 1990, use of natural gas is prohibited entirely, subject to certain partial exemptions. Funds are provided to aid utilities in setting up pollution controls and to reduce other negative impacts. Initially the Carter administration had also asked for a heavy tax on industrial use of oil and gas as a way to provide incentives for conversion, but that approach was dropped in conference after being watered down by the House and Senate.

Utility rate reform. Public utility rate reform standards were set up under the Public Utility Regulatory Policies Act of 1978 (H.R. 4018, P.L. 95-617). One set of six standards to encourage conservation is voluntary, but if states do not comply within three years, DOE could intervene in state proceedings to request compliance. State denial of DOE intervention in state proceedings would be grounds for DOE to seek compliance through the courts. The standards include prohibition of "declining bloc rates" and increased use of time-of-day, seasonal, and interruptible rates. A second set of standards oriented toward consumer protection as well as conservation are also voluntary but, if within two years the state regulatory agencies do not adopt them, a statement of reasons must be filed. Rate discrimination against alternative energy sources and master metering are prohibited, and procedures to protect against abrupt termination of service are required. The law also required that utilities set up programs to fund public participation in rate proceedings under certain conditions.

Conservation. A number of energy conservation measures other than tax incentives were provided for in the National Energy Conservation Policy Act (H.R. 5037, P.L. 95-619). Upon request, public utilities must provide estimates of the costs and amount of energy saved by the purchase and installation of conservation measures. The utilities must also inform their customers about what conservation measures are available. Public utilities must also offer to arrange for the financing and installation of these measures although they could not themselves sell or install them. Utilities must also allow customers to make payments on these improvements through their utility bills. In other sections of the law the civil fine on automobile manufacturers that exceeds the limits set for average gas mileage on a given fleet of cars is raised from $5 to $10 per car for every tenth of a mile per gallon that the fleet exceeds the limits subject to certain findings by the secretary of DOE. The Department of Energy is required to set up energy efficiency standards for thirteen categories of appliances, and large industrial users are required to report their energy consumption figures each year to DOE.

Energy taxes. Finally, a series of tax incentives for conservation were provided in the Energy Production and Conservations Tax Incentive Act (H.R. 5263, P.L. 95-618). Homeowners are eligible for a maximum nonrefundable tax credit of $300 on residential insulation and energy conservation measures. Investment in alternative power sources makes them eligible for another maximum credit of $2,200. A 10 percent investment tax credit would be available to business firms that installed certain types of energy-saving equipment and a favorable depreciation allowance provided for early retirement of oil and gas-fired boilers. Tax advantages are also provided for those who produce both conventional and unconventional energy such as geothermal energy. The most publicized part of the bill established a gradually escalating excise tax on the so-called gas guzzling automobiles that fall substantially below the federally mandated fleet mileage standards for each year. The administration had wanted the tax to start on 1978 models and be refundable to purchasers of energy-saving cars, but Congress ignored both requests. The tax will start on 1980 models and by 1986 apply to all cars getting less than 22.5 mpg. The administration had favored a 1986 figure of 27.5 mpg as the cut-off point for the tax.

Energy requests not enacted. Conspicuously missing from the energy legislation were two additional Carter administration requests—a wellhead tax on domestically produced crude oil to bring the price eventually up to world levels (some of which would be rebated to the public) and authority to add a 5 cent per gallon tax to gasoline each year until 1989 if domestic consumption exceeded certain specified levels. In addition, the negative tax aspects of the plan were generally less punitive than the White House had desired, and DOE powers to require adoption of different parts of the program were less than those requested.

In a related measure the Senate attempted to block the Energy Department from making good on its warning that it might impose a stiff $5 per barrel tax on imported oil (which is permitted under the 1962 Trade Expansion Act) if the tax on domestic oil failed to pass. In an amendment to a general appropriation bill (H.R. 12930), the Senate banned both import fees and import quotas. However, the House failed to accept the amendment.

Clean Air and Clean Water Amendments of 1977. By delaying the existing standards for automobile emissions for two years, the Clean Air Amendments (H.R. 6161, P.L. 95-95) in some sense relaxed regulation. However, the law also tightened standards for the 1980 and 1981 models. The law set new standards to implement the Environmental Protection Agency's policy of preventing significant deterioration in clean air areas but also set the system up so that some development can occur near these areas. The deadlines for cities to meet national air quality standards were extended until 1982 and in some cases to 1987, and most industrial polluters were allowed up to three more years to comply with clean air laws before facing heavy fines. Yet, the new source performance standards require new sources to make use of "the best technological system of continuous emission reduction" even if they use untreated low sulfur coal. Existing high altitude regulations were suspended until 1981, but penalties against those who tamper with emission control devices were increased.

The Clean Water Act of 1977 (H.R. 3199, P.L. 95-217) introduced by Ray Roberts (D-Tex.) and as S. 1952 by Edmund Muskie (D-Me.) was also ambivalent. Controls on toxic substances were increased. The requirement for formal hearings before EPA can add such a chemical to its list of those requiring standards was relaxed. It was also agreed to allow no waivers from clean-up requirements for toxics. However, deadlines were relaxed in several areas of compliance, and secondary treatment requirements for cities that dump their wastes into deep ocean waters were relaxed.

Federal Drug Regulation. The administration's drug regulatory reform bill (H.R. 11611, S. 2755), sponsored by Representatives Paul Rogers (D-Fla.) and Tim Lee Carter (R-Ky.) and Senator Kennedy, with nine cosponsors, was the outgrowth of over ten years of effort to alter the basic statutes governing the FDA. During the last decade nineteen formal reviews of the agency have been conducted. The latest concluded in May 1977 that the system of drug regulation established by the 1962 amendments was "fundamentally sound" despite the need for some improvements. In recent years a proposal by Senator Kennedy called for the FDA to be separated from HEW. A proposal by Senator Nelson advocated an independent board to evaluate drug company test results, and a measure filed by Representative Steven Symms (R-Idaho) with nineteen cosponsors, H.R. 54, advocated elimination of the efficacy requirements which prevent drugs like laetrile from being certified. Bills similar to the Symms measure had 115 cosponsors.

The administration bill, the Drug Regulation Reform Act of 1978, would not follow any of these approaches, but it did make some important changes in FDA procedures for approval of new drugs. First, it would have established what are known as "drug treatment investigations" for experimentation on human participants with a serious disease who cannot be satisfactorily served by alternative methods. Informal consent must have been obtained from the patients and elaborate criteria governed the process, but this system would have helped get new drugs more easily to patients in life or death situations. Second, the definition of drug effectiveness was relaxed in certain situations so that drugs could have been issued provisionally. Third, procedures that encourage public participation were added. Fourth, the establishment of a Federal Clinical Pharmacology Center would have helped in the testing of drugs with low profit and thus helped get these drugs tested and approved. Fifth, the pill bottle inserts containing information on side effects (which would have been required under the law) might have encouraged the FDA to take the political risks of issuing drugs more quickly. Sixth, barriers to entry would also have been reduced. After five years of exclusive use of a new drug by its inventor, others would not have had to do duplicate safety testing from scratch. This would have lowered the costs of entry.

On the other hand, the FDA could more easily have removed from the market the drugs it found hazardous. Under the previous system the FDA had to prove such a drug was an "imminent" hazard to the nation's health, a standard so difficult to prove that it was successfully used only once. This was changed to "unreasonable and substantial risk of illness."

Other sections of the bill also pointed in opposite directions as far as the relaxing of regulation is concerned. The existing drug export laws were loosened, but new restrictions were placed on drug advertising and criminal penalties were increased.

APPENDIX A: BOX SCORE OF REGULATORY BILLS

Passed Congress or Enacted

S. Res. 4	Economic impact statement to accompany reported bills	Adopted as Senate rule
H.R. 11445	OSHA exemptions for small business	Vetoed
S. 555	Financial disclosure of government officials	P.L. 95-521
S. 2796	Amendments to Consumer Product Safety Commission Act	P.L. 95-631
S. 3084	Duplicative paperwork in federal housing program	P.L. 95-557
S. 2570	Elimination of paperwork in CETA program	P.L. 95-524
S. 2493	Airline deregulation	P.L. 95-504
S. 2899	Modification of Endangered Species Act	P.L. 95-632
S. 1750	Delay of saccharin ban	P.L. 95-203
S. 1678	Modification of pesticide registration law	P.L. 95-396
H.R. 5383	Expansion of mandatory retirement protection	P.L. 95-256
S. 1503	Reimbursement for Tris-treated clothes manufacturers	Vetoed
H.R. 5289	Regulation of intrastate natural gas and long-term deregulation of new gas	P.L. 95-621
H.R. 5146	Coal conversion program	P.L. 95-620
H.R. 4018	Utility rate reforms	P.L. 95-617
H.R. 5037	Conservation of energy	P.L. 95-619
H.R. 5263	Energy taxes	P.L. 95-618
H.R. 6161	Clean air amendments	P.L. 95-95
H.R. 3199	Water pollution amendments	P.L. 95-217
H.R. 14279	Omnibus banking regulation	P.L. 95-630
S. 305	Overseas business payments	P.L. 95-213
H.R. 2	Strip mining controls	P.L. 95-87

H.R. 8638	Nuclear export controls	P.L. 95-242
S. 9	Outer continental shelf leasing	P.L. 95-372
H.R. 4297	Ocean dumping amendments	P.L. 95-153
S. 682	Tanker safety law	P.L. 95-474
H.R. 13650	Uranium mill waste disposal	P.L. 95-604
H.R. 10899	Regulation of foreign banks	P.L. 95-369
S. 717	Mine safety amendments	P.L. 95-164
S. 1185	Off-track betting regulation	P.L. 95-515
H.R. 5294	Regulation of debt collection practices	P.L. 95-109
H.R. 7442	Regulation of cable television utility pole hook-up	P.L. 95-234
S. 2401	Home insulation standard	P.L. 95-319
H.R. 130	Gas station dealer day in court	P.L. 95-297
H.R. 12930	Ban on gun control regulations	P.L. 95-429
H.R. 2521	Rabbit meat inspection	Vetoed
H.R. 11545	Restrictions on lifting of beef import quotas and new import formula	Vetoed
H.R. 9518	Penalties for illegal shipping rebates	Vetoed

Bills That Failed to Pass Congress

H.R. 10257	Statutory requirements for economic impact statements	Died in committee
S. 3549 H.R. 14369	Extend executive order on regulatory reform to independent agencies	Died in committee
H.R. 14339	Establish Office of Regulatory Review in GAO	Died in committee
S. 3366 H.R. 13723	Require presidential ranking of programs	Passed Senate as amendment to S. 2 (sunset)
H.R. 351	Require cost/benefit assessments	Died in committee
S. 3262 H.R. 14370	Require 5 percent reduction in compliance costs	Died in committee
S. 3550 H.R. 14370	Establish regulatory budget	Died in committee
S. 1199	Allow President to delay implementation of a regulation	Died in committee
S. 1974	Flexibility in applying regulations to small business	Passed Senate
H.R. 959	Legislative veto of agency regulations	Died in committee

H.R. 960	Legislative veto of agency rules without retroactive feature	Died in committee
H.R. 961	Legislative veto of agency rules with economic and criminal penalties	Died in committee
H.R. 116 S. 1463	Legislative veto of agency regulations	Died in committee
H.R. 4901	Legislative veto of agency regulations	Died in committee
S. 2011 H.R. 11006	Legislative veto of agency regulations with cost/benefit required	Died in committee
S. 2862	Legislative veto attached to all new laws and reviews required every 5 years	Died in committee
S. 3629	Legislative veto of agency rules including a Joint Committee on Administrative Rules	Died in committee
H.R. 14222	Legislative veto of agency rules with Joint Committee on Administrative Rules	Died in committee
S. 1721	Administrative reforms: notice and comment, delay	Died in committee
H.R. 5633	Administrative reforms: notice and comment and legislative veto	Died in committee
H.R. 2416	Administrative reforms: notice and comment and grant-in-aid procedures	Died in committee
H.R. 2586	Administrative reforms, cost/ benefit, attorney's fees	Died in committee
S. 3240	Reforms to increase independence of regulatory agencies and reduce conflicts of interest	Died in committee
S. 1532, S. 1534-1536	Independent regulatory agency reforms	Passed Senate
H.R. 3518	Establish nominating board for regulatory appointments	Died in committee
H.R. 8494	Lobbying disclosure	Passed House
H.R. 3816 S. 1288	FTC amendments	Passed House and Senate; House re-jected conference report twice
S. 1262 H.R. 6805 and H.R. 9718	Establish agency for consumer protection	Reported by Senate; defeated on House floor
S. 270 H.R. 3361 and H.R. 8798	Payment of attorney's fees for public participation	Died in committee

H.R. 2104	Payment of attorney's fees for public participation concerning 3 pieces of legislation	Died in committee
S. 3475	General class action bill	Died in committee
S. 1874	Reversal of *Illinois Brick* v. *Illinois* (antitrust suits by indirect purchasers)	Reported by Senate
S. 3263 H.R. 14166	Eliminate conflicting regulations	Passed Senate as amendment to S. 2 (sunset)
H.R. 284 H.R. 640 and H.R. 2616	Establish National Commission on Regulatory Reform	Died in committee
S. 1720	Administrative reforms: delay and expedited procedures	Died in committee
S. 2490	Administrative reforms: delay and expedited procedures	Died in committee
S. 2625	Establish standard to eliminate anticompetitive regulation	Died in committee
S. 2	Sunset of all federal programs	Passed Senate
S. 600	Establish procedure for sunset review of regulatory programs	Passed Senate as amendment to S. 2
S. 1244	Budget reauthorization	Died in committee
H.R. 10421	Sunset without automatic termination	Died in committee
H.R. 3411	Sunset of specific regulatory agencies	Died in committee
H.R. 3181	Sunset of specific regulatory agencies	Died in committee
S. 292	Airline deregulation	Died in committee
H.R. 9297	Modified airline deregulation	Died in committee
H.R. 13015	Communications partial deregulation	Died in committee
S. 2374	Expedite ICC procedures	Died in committee
S. 547	Change ICC procedures for surface transportation	Died in committee
S. 2269	Allow exemptions from ICC procedures	Died in committee
S. 2443	Exempt independent truckers from certain ICC procedures	Died in committee

S. 2307	Limit charges of household movers	Died in committee
H.R. 11327	Delay pending ban on nitrites	Died in committee
S. 2055	Legalize NOW checking accounts	Reported in Senate
H.R. 13553	Kazen Amendment to allow exchange of coal leases	Defeated on House floor vote
S. 2775 H.R. 11704	Nuclear licensing reforms	Died in committee
H.R. 11611 S. 2755	Drug regulation reform	Died in committee
H.R. 54	Repeal of FDA efficacy requirements	Died in committee
H.R. 8410 S. 2467	Labor law revisions	Passed House; died in Senate filibuster
H.R. 4250	Common-site picketing	Defeated in vote on House floor
H.R. 1037	Oil tanker cargo preference	Defeated in vote on House floor
S. 1381 H.R. 13048	No-fault auto insurance standards	Defeated in House committee vote
H.R. 6575 S. 1391	Hospital cost containment	Passed Senate in modified form as amendment to S. 1470; died in House
S. 2410 H.R. 11488	Health planning	Passed Senate; House version failed under suspension of the rules
H.R. 11192 Amdt. 1713 to S. 1217	DNA regulation	Died in committee
H.R. 13175	Accounting profession self-regulation	Died in committee
H.R. 9505 S. 2193	Automatic telephone dialing machine regulation	Died in committee
S. 705	Clinical lab standards	Died in committee
H.R. 11622 S. 1895	Liquefied natural gas controls	House passed as part of S. 1895; Senate refused to go to conference
H.R. 3350 S. 2053	Seabed mining licenses	Passed House; reported by Senate

APPENDIX B:
ADDITIONAL BILLS WITH REGULATORY IMPLICATIONS

Customs Law Reforms—H.R. 8149, P.L. 95-410
Modernized and simplified U.S. customs laws; raised duty-free allowance.

Bankruptcy Law Reform—H.R. 8200, P.L. 95-598
Established a bankruptcy court system; provided increased protection to debtors.

Investor Protection—H.R. 8331, P.L. 283
Doubled the amount of investor's cash and securities that could be insured by Securities Investor Protection Corporation to protect against broker liquidation.

Black Lung Benefits—H.R. 4544, P.L. 95-239
Established more lenient rules to determine eligibility for benefits.

Black Lung Benefits—H.R. 5322, P.L. 95-227
Imposed excise taxes on coal sales to fund benefits program.

Waterway User Fees—H.R. 8533, P.L. 95-502
Imposed tax on fuel used by inland waterway barges.

Safe Drinking Water—S. 1528, P.L. 95-190
Granted the states a waiver from requirement that they assume primary enforcement responsibility for public water systems.

Minimum Wage Increase—H.R. 3744, P.L. 95-151
Increased minimum wage in four-step process to $3.35 by 1981.

Consumer Co-op Bank—H.R. 2777, P.L. 95-351
Established a bank to make loans to nonprofit consumer cooperatives.

Farm Credit—H.R. 11504, P.L. 95-334
Reorganized and increased farm loan programs.

Civil Service Reform—S. 2640, P.L. 95-454
Established bonus system for government executives; liberalized dismissal rules.

Humphrey-Hawkins Full Employment—H.R. 50, P.L. 95-523
Established national goal of reducing unemployment rate to 3 percent by 1985 and eliminating it by 1988.

Marine Mammal Protection—S. 1522, P.L. 95-136
Reauthorized the 1972 bill and banned whaling within 200 mile offshore limit.

Redwoods Lands—H.R. 3813, P.L. 95-250
Authorized the purchase of 48,000 acres of privately owned redwoods timberlands for placement in Redwood National Park. Provided compensation to timber workers who lose their jobs due to the law.

Grazing Fee System—H.R. 10587, P.L. 95-514
Set up a new grazing fee system that would reduce charges to ranchers when beef prices were low.

Noise Control Reauthorization—S. 3083, P.L. 95-609
Reauthorized 1972 noise control program and required that FAA respond to EPA's proposed aviation noise rules.

Oil Spill Liability—H.R. 6803, S. 2083
Would have increased the liability of those responsible for oil spills and set up a fund to pay clean-up costs. Whether to cover hazardous chemicals as well as oil was in dispute in the Senate. Passed the House, reported in the Senate.

Coal Slurry Pipelines—H.R. 1609
Would have granted pipelines carrying coal slurry the right of way to cross land owned by railroads and the power of eminent domain. Opposed by railroads because it was competitive form of transportation. Defeated in floor vote in the House.

Alaska Land Conservation—H.R. 39
Would have restricted development of millions of acres of wilderness land and added much of it to the national park system. Passed House, died in Senate because of threatened filibuster.

Sugar Production—H.R. 13750
Would have authorized U.S. participation in international sugar agreement and reauthorized import quotas and fees to increase price of domestic sugar. House rejected conference.

Subsidized Crop Insurance—H.R. 7111
Would have replaced current crop insurance system with new subsidized program. Died in committee.

Consumer Dispute Resolution—S. 957
Would have provided assistance to the states to help set up procedures for resolving minor consumer-business disputes. Passed Senate, failed in House under suspension of the rules.

Aviation Noise—H.R. 8729, S. 3279
Would have authorized surcharges on airfares to help airlines pay for retrofitting of engines to reduce noise. Passed House, died in Senate committee.

Hatch Act Reform—H.R. 10
Would have repealed many of the restrictions on political activity by federal government employees. Passed House, died in Senate committee.

NOTES

[1] Congressional Reference Service, Library of Congress, "Congressional Review, Deferral and Disapproval of Executive Action: A Summary and an Inventory of Statutory Authority," April 30, 1976, and "1976–1977 Congressional Acts Authorizing Prior Review, Approval or Disapproval of Proposed Executive Actions," May 25, 1978.

[2] Congressional Reference Service, Library of Congress, "Interim Report on the Exercise of Congressional Review, Deferral and Disapproval Authority over Proposed Executive Actions, 1960–1975," and telephone interview with Clark Norton, Congressional Research Service, November 20, 1978.

[3] See "The Specter of the Legislative Veto," *National Journal,* September 30, 1978, p. 1561.